INDIANS OF IDAHO

Other books by Deward E. Walker, Jr. from the
University of Idaho Press

Conflict & Schism in Nez Perce Acculturation:
A Study of Religion and Politics

Myths of Idaho Indians

(ed.) Systems of North American Witchcraft
and Sorcery

INDIANS OF IDAHO
DEWARD E. WALKER, JR.

UNIVERSITY OF IDAHO PRESS
MOSCOW, IDAHO

©1978 by The Idaho Research Foundation, Inc.
Published by The University of Idaho Press
3368 University Station
Moscow, Idaho 83843

Printed in the United States of America
9 8 7 6 5 4

ISBN 0-89301-053-7
Library of Congress Catalog Card number 78-52574

An Anthropological Monograph of
the University of Idaho
Roderick Sprague, Editor

TABLE OF CONTENTS

PREFACE

Many people have aided in the preparation of this volume. John Tokle, a graduate student in anthropology at the University of Idaho, helped gather the published information on aboriginal cultural patterns. Harold Farley and Max Snow of the Idaho State Department of Education are to be commended for recognizing the need for this volume and securing the necessary funds for its completion.

I also wish to acknowledge the kind assistance of Professor Sven Liljeblad of Idaho State University, who permitted me to consult his voluminous notes on the aboriginal cultures of southern Idaho. The staff of the University of Idaho and Washington State University libraries also provided valuable assistance in locating many rare publications.

Judith Magee deserves special thanks for her patient, thorough typing and her critical review of the manuscript. Finally, Dr. Roderick Sprague has provided valuable advice and essential assistance in getting this book printed.

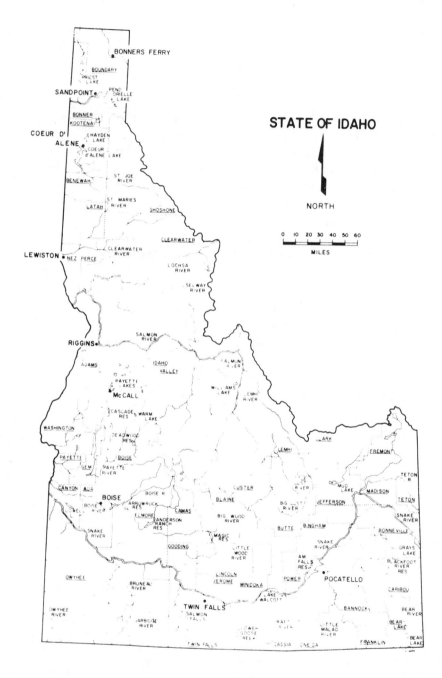

Fig. 1. State of Idaho.

CHAPTER 1

INTRODUCTION

This book is a general survey of the aboriginal American Indian cultures of Idaho and summarizes most of the anthropological and historical writings on the native peoples of this region. It is prompted by a growing public and professional interest in Native American cultures, and is designed for teachers, students, and all those interested in Idaho's native peoples. It is not written for the professional anthropologist and **does not** deal with contemporary Indian cultures of the State of Idaho, which have been drastically transformed by treaties, reservations, missionaries, loss of native languages, and Euro-American education. The six aboriginal cultures described are the Kutenai, Kalispel, Coeur d'Alene, Nez Perce, Shoshone-Bannock and Northern Paiute. This information will enable teachers to prepare units of instruction in American Indian cultures for their students.

ETHNOLOGY

This book is written from the point of view of *ethnology*, or as it is sometimes called, cultural anthropology. The work of the ethnologist begins where the work of the archaeologist ends, i.e., ethnologists study recent or modern cultures. *Ethnographies*, the writings of ethnologists, can be either historical reconstructions of recent cultures or descriptions of contemporary cultures. They usually begin with a description of the natural environment and then proceed to describe social institutions such as the economy, social organization, and religion. Ethnographies usually contain many chapters and sometimes extend to several thousand pages. The techniques used by ethnologists to reconstruct aboriginal cultural patterns among American Indians have usually included learning the native language, relying primarily on elderly informants whose knowledge of the past is reliable, frequent cross-checking of information among informants, and careful use of theoretical and comparative materials drawn from neighboring, closely related groups. When feasible, findings of archaeologists are used as well as historical documents left by early explorers, fur traders, missionaries, and the native peoples themselves.

In Idaho we are fortunate to have several excellent ethnographic accounts, completed early in this century, using informants who remembered the aboriginal life patterns. These early ethnographies are invaluable to us, and the majority of the information in this book is drawn from these pioneering works.

SOURCES

Some might say that ethnology in Idaho begins with the observations of the first explorers, fur traders, missionaries, and government agents to enter the area. Although they sometimes made highly accurate observations, in most cases these writings lack accuracy and comprehension. Although there are exceptions, they usually present a prejudiced, naive, ethnocentric viewpoint, wherein the writer sees his own Euro-American culture as vastly superior to the native cultures. Many of the earlier writings of ethnologists are also inadequate and lack the insights of more recent works. Thus, caution must be exercised when drawing on many published materials dealing with the native peoples of Idaho and American Indians in general.

A number of highly reliable ethnological works on aboriginal American Indians have become available in recent years. These deal with the United States and North America as a whole, although most contain some useful materials on Idaho. References to them are included in the general bibliography. Driver (1961), Murdock (1960, 1967), Spencer, Jennings, et al. (1965), Oswalt (1966), Underhill (1953, 1965), Walker (1971), and Eggan (1955) probably are the best general reference works now available. Swanson (1970) has edited a useful book on native cultures of the Northwest. Published ethnological works on the aboriginal cultures of Idaho are much more difficult to obtain. Many are either out of print or published in journals not usually available in local libraries. However, most can be obtained by your local librarian, thanks to the interlibrary loan program. If the original sources are to be consulted, this procedure is required.

The most comprehensive general ethnography on the Kutenai is by Turney-High (1941a). This ethnography includes information on Kutenai history and intergroup relations, natural environment, technology and subsistence activities, housing, transportation, clothing, individual life cycle, family and political organization, art, and religion. Baker (1955) briefly covers the same topics as Turney-High and adds substantial materials on acculturation and present conditions. Jenness (1932) covers most of the material contained in Turney-High and Baker, but only superficially. Additional notes on the Kutenai will be found in the many earlier publications of the pioneers Wilson (1890) and Chamberlain (1893, 1893-95, 1894, 1901a, 1901b, 1901c, 1902, 1905, 1907, 1909). Ray (1942) wrote a useful ethnographic summary on the Kutenai, and Boas (1918) is the major source on Kutenai mythology. Ewers (1955) makes occasional comments on Kutenai horse culture.

The principal published ethnography on the Kalispel is by James Teit (1930). He describes them as part of what he calls the "Flathead Group" which includes the Flathead, Pend d'Oreille, and Kalispel. Information is included on their history and intergroup relations, natural environment, technology and subsistence activities, housing, transportation, clothing, individual life cycles, family and political organization, art, and religion. An interesting master's thesis containing information on Kalispel kinship and family organization was written by Bahar (n.d.). Ray (1942) also summarizes most of the available ethnographic information on the Kalispel, and Teit (1917a, 1917b) and Vogt (1940) are major sources on Kalispel mythology.

James Teit (1930) describes the Coeur d'Alene with much the same ethnographic information he presents for the Kalispel. The master's theses of Dozier (n.d.) and Stevens (n.d.) also contain much useful information. Gladys Reichard (1930, 1947) and James Teit (1917a) have published extensively on Coeur d'Alene myths, and Ewers (1955) presents some information on the uses of the horse among the Coeur d'Alene. Ray (1942) has given us a useful ethnographic summary of this group.

Most readers will know the Nez Perces through historians

such as Haines (1938, 1955) and Josephy (1965). Fortunately, an increasing number of ethnologists are turning their attention to the Nez Perces. Lundsgaarde (n.d.) describes kinship and family organization, and Schwede (n.d.) concentrates on settlement patterns. Spinden (1908) presents information covered in traditional ethnographies — natural environment, technology and subsistence activities, housing, transportation, clothing, individual life cycles, family and political organization, art, and religion. Walker (1964, 1966, 1967a, 1967b, 1968a, 1968b) adds to Spinden's observations on political organization, religion, subsistence and technology, and Ewers (1955) presents some valuable information on Nez Perce horse culture. We are particularly fortunate in having a large number of published Nez Perce myths of a Nez Perce anthropologist, Archie Phinney (1934).

Robert Lowie (1909, 1915, 1919, 1924a, 1924b) is a major contributor to the ethnography of the aboriginal Shoshone-Bannock, providing information on territory, technology and subsistence activities, family and political organization, religion, art, and mythology. Julian Steward (1936, 1938a, 1938b, 1955) also provides extensive ethnographic information on the Northern Shoshone and many other groups in the Great Basin. Steward concentrates particularly on environment, subsistence and technology, population density, settlement patterns, and family political organization. More recently, Cappannari (n.d.) has summarized and interpreted the information dealing with property concepts among the Shoshone. Similar information on the closely allied Bannock will be found in Steward (1938a) and Madsen (n.d.). Other useful sources are Downs (1966), Fowler (1966), Stewart (1966), and Swanson (1966), all of whom are included in the recent symposium on anthropological research in the Great Basin (d'Azevedo, et al. 1966). Ewers (1955) presents a limited amount of information on Shoshone-Bannock horse culture.

Omer Stewart (1937, 1939b, 1941, 1944) has been a major contributor to Northern Paiute ethnography. His publications include information on territory, environment, subsistence activities, family and political organization, housing, clothing, transportation, and religion. His 1939a publication focuses

14

primarily on political organization. Julian Steward (1938a) also deals with Northern Paiute environment, political and family organization, technology and subsistence activities, and population. Another very important contributor is Whiting (1950) who concentrates on the Harney Valley division of the Northern Paiute. Although she heavily emphasizes religion, social control, and sorcery, she also includes much information on the individual life cycle and subsistence activities. Willard Park (1937) also focuses on Northern Paiute religion, and Ruth Underhill (1941) gives a general summary of the aboriginal ethnography of the Northern Paiute. Isabel Kelly (1939) is a good source for Northern Paiute myths.

ORGANIZATION

It will be noted in the following description of aboriginal life in Idaho that the quantity and quality of the information varies slightly from one group to another. Although we have obtained generally equivalent ethnographic information for each group, there are some unavoidable gaps in the available published materials. Some groups have had excellent descriptions written of their subsistence patterns, but have suffered very superficial accounts of religion and family life, and vice versa. Despite these occasional limitations in source materials, we believe the following description of Idaho's aboriginal cultures to be generally representative and well-balanced.

Chapter 2 contains a description of the principal natural and cultural areas existing in Idaho about A.D. 1800-1850. This is followed by a description of the aboriginal life patterns of Idaho's native peoples in terms of subsistence (Chapter 3), social organization (Chapter 4), and world view (Chapter 5). Chapters 3 and 4 present the information by tribe. This way, the reader can focus on particular groups if he wishes, and compare the ways in which the tribes were similar and unique. Because of the limited amount of research on religion and mythology in aboriginal Idaho, we were unable to present the information in Chapter 5 by tribe. What we have presented is a general description which is applicable in most respects to Idaho's aboriginal cultures. Nevertheless, there were variations in world view, as seen in religion and mythology, and for those interested in reading more about them, we suggest that the basic sources in the bibliography be consulted.

CHAPTER 2

NATURAL AND CULTURAL AREAS OF IDAHO

The present State of Idaho (Figure 1) contains approximately 83,557 square miles. It possesses natural and cultural diversity as great as any part of the United States, a fact which becomes readily apparent when traveling the length of Idaho. The north's wooded land with its many lakes and rivers changes to rolling grassland as one moves south, and becomes desert by the time the southern border is reached.

Anthropologists in Idaho and neighboring areas have extensively researched the question of how cultural patterns reflect the natural environment; this field of investigation is called *cultural ecology*. Over many thousands of years the aboriginal inhabitants of Idaho continuously adapted their activities to their natural environment. Because of their relatively simple hunting and gathering mode of life, Idaho's aboriginal inhabitants were deeply affected by changes of temperature and precipitation as well as changes of fauna and flora. Consequently, changes in the seasons required people to move from one area to another. During winter most groups concentrated in protected locations at lower elevations, whereas in summer many dispersed into the highlands. Even houses, tools, and population densities were influenced by shifts in the natural environment. A number of maps follow which will acquaint the reader with the diversity of Idaho's aboriginal natural and cultural regions.

Figure 2 shows the major drainage basins in Idaho, and Figure 3 shows the Indian tribes of Idaho. As can be seen, the tribes are closely identified with the various drainage basins. The aboriginal territories of the Kutenai, the Kalispel, and the Coeur d'Alene tribes are closely identified, respectively, with the Kutenai, Pend d'Oreille, and Spokane drainages, all of which empty into the Columbia River. The Palouse, Clearwater, and Salmon drainage basins are drained by rivers of the same names

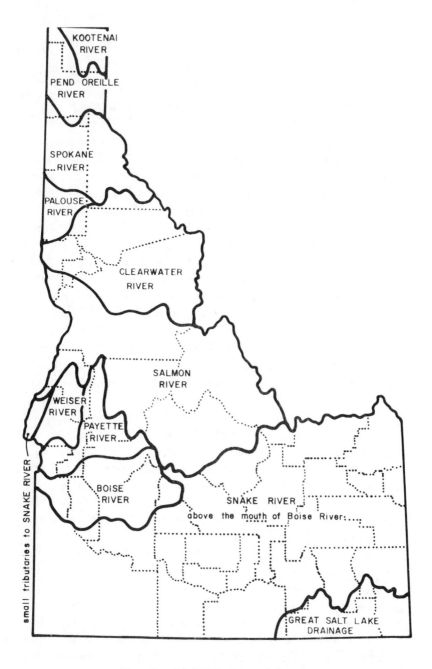

Fig. 2. Idaho drainage basins.

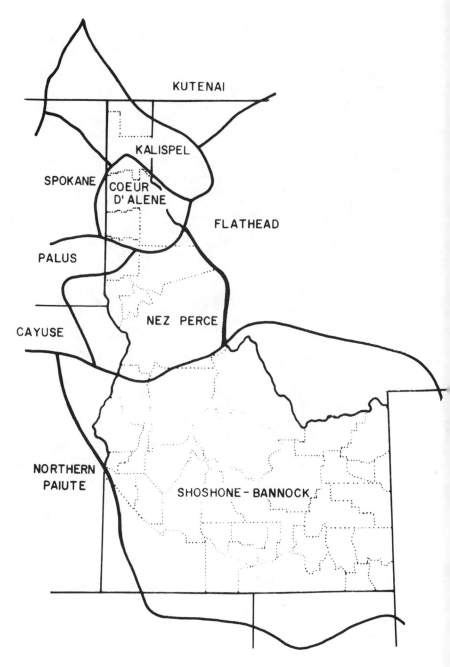

Fig. 3. Indian tribes of Idaho.

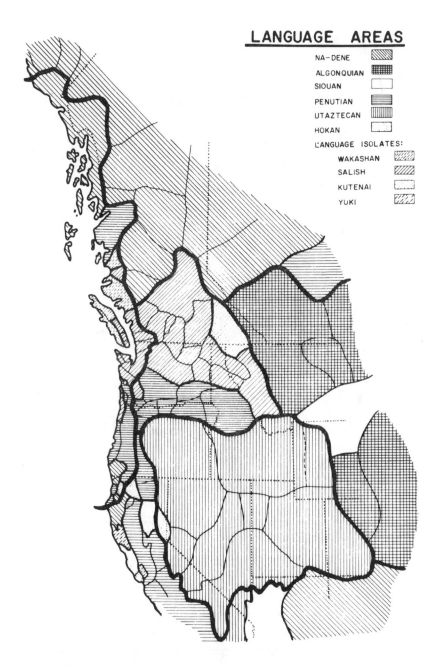

LANGUAGE AREAS

NA-DENE
ALGONQUIAN
SIOUAN
PENUTIAN
UTAZTECAN
HOKAN
LANGUAGE ISOLATES:
WAKASHAN
SALISH
KUTENAI
YUKI

Fig. 4. Language areas, northwestern North America.

20

and empty into the middle Snake River. This area encompasses primarily the aboriginal territory of the Nez Perces. The Weiser, Payette, Boise, and Snake (above the mouth of the Boise River) drainage basins empty into the upper Snake River. The Northern Paiute bands of Idaho were located in the western portion of these drainages, whereas the Shoshone-Bannock groups were located in the eastern portion. The Shoshone-Bannock dominated the Snake River drainage above the mouth of the Boise River and a small portion of the Great Salt Lake drainage found in the southeastern corner of the state. Thus, there is a close correspondence between the home territories of Idaho's aboriginal peoples and the various river drainage basins.

Figure 4 shows the major language groupings of aboriginal Idaho, which also correspond closely to the same natural divisions of the region. For example, the northernmost drainage basin, the Kutenai, contains speakers of the Kutenai language which some scholars think is related to the vast Algonquian language stock which extends across the Great Plains into eastern North America. The Pend d'Oreille and Spokane drainage basins were occupied by speakers of Interior Salishan languages. These languages extend from eastern Montana up into Canada and down to the Pacific coasts of Washington and Oregon. The Palouse, Clearwater, and northern portion of the Salmon river drainage basins were inhabited by speakers of the Nez Perce language which is closely related to other Sahaptian languages to the west, such as Umatilla and Yakima, and ultimately joins with the Penutian languages of California. The remaining drainage basins located in southern Idaho all were occupied by speakers of languages belonging to the Shoshonean language family, itself part of the vast Utaztecan stock extending south deep into central Mexico.

Anthropological linguists classify language groupings from the largest to the smallest units, i.e., stocks, families, languages, and dialects. Aboriginal Idaho contained at least two stocks, Penutian and Utaztecan. As indicated in Figure 5, doubt still remains as to the proper stock affiliation of Kutenai and Salish. Aboriginal Idaho also contained representatives of at least four language families, Kutenai, Salish (both of which are isolates with no known related families), Sahaptian, and Numic. The

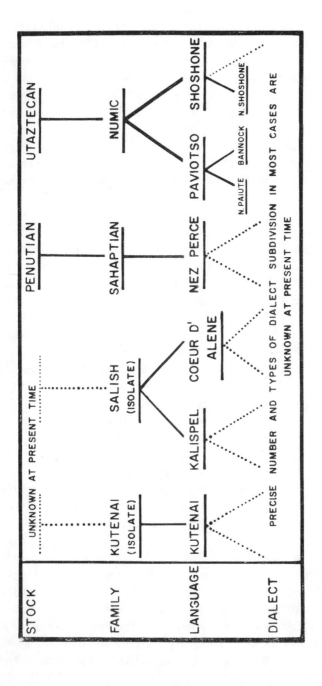

Fig. 5. Language relationships among Indians of Idaho.

Sahaptian family contains the Nez Perce language in Idaho and the Sahaptin language in neighboring Oregon and Washington, the latter being divided into a number of dialects such as Yakima and Umatilla. The Northern Paiute and Bannock are closely related dialects of a language belonging to the Numic family. The Shoshone language also belongs to the Numic family, and is divided into a number of dialects including Northern Shoshone. Therefore, aboriginal Idaho contained at least two language stocks, four language families, and six different languages. As suggested in the diagram (Figure 5), these languages were subdivided into a number of dialects. For the most part, these dialects were distinct, but mutually intelligible. For example, there is about the same degree of difference between the Bannock and Northern Paiute dialects as there is between English as spoken in New England and in the Southeastern United States.

It is clear, therefore, that statements about American Indians speaking different *dialects* is a gross over-simplification. In Idaho this is particularly true. For example, the difference between the Penutian and Utaztecan stocks may be as great as that between the Sino-Tibetan and Indo-European stocks in the Old World. In order to appreciate the linguistic diversity of Idaho's aboriginal inhabitants, one need only consider that at least a century is normally required for a language to sub-divide into dialects, at least one thousand years is required for dialects to become languages, i.e., sufficiently distinct to be mutually unintelligible. The differences between Idaho's six distinct languages represent thousands of years of separate development. Ongoing archaeological research is also confirming the great antiquity (at least 12,000 years) of Idaho's aboriginal cultures.

The reader may wonder how such marked language differences were overcome. Simply put, the aboriginal inhabitants of Idaho and North America generally were multilingual, i.e., they knew several often quite dissimilar languages. Children were sometimes sent to live with other groups so they could learn their languages. A *lingua franca*, Chinook Jargon, also was used in the aboriginal Northwest, primarily for trade, but in other transactions also. A highly developed sign language also aided communication between

PRINCIPAL INDIAN GROUPS AND CULTURAL AREAS

1. COMOX
2. LILLOOET
3. THOMPSON
4. NICOLA
5. OKANOGAN
6. COWICHAN
7. KLALLAM
8. TWANA
9. SNUQUALMI
10. SANPOIL
11. KALISPEL
12. SPOKANE
13. COEUR d'ALENE
14. CHEHALIS
15. CHINOOK
16. KLIKITAT
17. WISHRAM
18. WALLAWALLA-PALUS
19. TENINO
20. MOLALA
21. UMATILLA
22. TAKELMA
23. KAROK
24. HUPA
25. KALAPUYA
26. KLAMATH
27. SHASTA
28. MODOC
29. WINTUN
30. ACHOMAWI
31. MAIDU
32. MIWOK

Fig. 6. Principal Indian groups and cultural areas, northwestern North America.

24

speakers of different languages throughout Idaho. Of course, today English has become the common language of American Indians in Idaho and most of North America. In the earliest phases of Euro-American exploration of the region, the native inhabitants of northern Idaho often learned French. A residue of this influence may be found in the many French loan words in Kutenai, Kalispel, Coeur d'Alene, and Nez Perce. Even Spanish loan words are encountered in the languages of southern Idaho.

Culturally, Idaho may be divided into two distinct areas. As Figure 6 indicates, the groups of northern and central Idaho were affiliated with other Plateau groups, such as the Yakima, while the aboriginal groups of southern Idaho were part of the Great Basin culture area, which also included the Ute and Paiute. The tribes contained in each culture area generally resembled one another in environmental adaptations and to a lesser extent in languages.

The Plateau culture area, which included the aboriginal tribes of northern and central Idaho, has many distinct features including the following:

1. Location in the environmentally diverse region between the Bitterroot and Cascade mountain ranges and between central British Columbia and central Oregon and Idaho.
2. Adaptation to a riverine environment with water craft and elaborate fishing technology which provided about half of the food base. Remaining food was secured from large game animals and relatively abundant tuberous roots. Most of the time there was a comfortable margin of survival in this culture area.
3. Intensive interaction between local groups based on kinship, trade, and political ties facilitated by either common language, multilingualism, or a trade language.
4. Band and composite band political organization (see Chapter 4), bilateral kinship, polygyny, primarily patrilocal residence, local communities rarely larger than 100 individuals, and winter residence in the major river valleys in semisubterranean houses.
5. Emphasis on democratic and peaceful interpersonal and intergroup relations.
6. Shaman-centered religions (see Chapter 5) with an

emphasis on the individual vision quest for a tutelary spirit, annual observance of first fruits and first salmon ceremonies, and a winter tutelary spirit dance.

Because of their location in Idaho on the eastern edge of the Plateau culture area, the aboriginal cultures of northern and central Idaho are somewhat atypical of general Plateau cultural patterns. Although they share many basic patterns of the Plateau, their interaction with inhabitants of the Great Plains culture area, after the introduction of the horse (about A.D. 1700), caused them to adopt many Plains culture traits. They came to extol the virtues of warfare, and they honored skilled warriors as *war leaders*. They also organized themselves into larger political groups primarily to defend themselves in warfare when out on the western Great Plains. Despite increasing dependence on bison, fishing remained important in the eastern Plateau, although not as important as in the central Plateau where it was still a major food source.

The Great Basin culture area, which included the southern Idaho tribes, was quite distinct culturally from the Plateau area. Distinguishing features of this large culture area included the following:

1. Location in a desiccated region with inland drainage into brackish lakes between the Mohave Desert on the south and southern Oregon and Idaho on the north, and between the eastern boundary of present California and central Wyoming.
2. Adaptation to a desert environment with intensive exploitation of nuts, seeds, roots, cactus, insects, small game animals, birds, and occasional large game. The margin of survival was thin, resulting in occasional starvation and frequent movement in search of food.
3. Limited interaction between groups except immediate neighbors.
4. Band political organization (see Chapter 4), bilateral kinships, polygyny and polyandry, primarily patrilocal or bilocal residence, occasional infanticide and senilicide, local communities rarely larger than thirty individuals, and residence near water resources in oases and at higher elevations.

5. Strong preference for democratic, peaceful behavior; little emphasis on warfare or other hostile intergroup relations.
6. Shaman-centered religions (see Chapter 5) with emphasis on the individual vision quest for a tutelary spirit and observance of seasonal ceremonies thought to increase the food supply.

Like the aboriginal cultures of northern and central Idaho, the Shoshone-Bannock and Northern Paiute inhabitants of southern Idaho were in many respects atypical of the Great Basin culture area. Two factors account for this difference in culture patterns, 1) their location on the upper Snake River, and 2) their proximity to the Plains culture area. Although technologically simplified when compared to the cultures of the Plateau, the Shoshone-Bannock of Idaho were rich by general Great Basin standards. Unlike most Great Basin tribes, they drew on the annual salmon runs and the game, birds, and edible plants in the productive Boise River and Salmon River drainage basins. By the time Euro-Americans arrived in the area, the Shoshone-Bannock already had the horse and had been deeply influenced by Plains culture. In fact, they had come to resemble the more northern Upper Kutenai, Kalispel, Coeur d'Alene, and Nez Perces who regularly visited the western Plains. They came to extol bravery in battle, count coup, and accorded successful warriors great honor and political power. They also lived in larger communities and organized themselves into composite band political groupings. All these differences plus their wealth in horses sharply separated the Shoshone-Bannock from their Northern Paiute neighbors to the west.

The information presented in Figures 7 through 11 indicates the great environmental differences between northern and central Idaho and southern Idaho. The boundary separating biotic zones 1 and 2 from biotic zone 3 (Figure 9) approximates the line separating the Plateau and the Great Basin culture areas in Idaho. Zone 1, the so-called northern Rocky Mountain biotic area, is mountainous, traversed by many rivers, and dotted with lakes. As much as 60 inches of precipitation, much of it snow, may fall in a single year (Figure 8), and temperature variations are mild (Figures 9 and 10). Many types of coniferous trees are found here, e.g., western white pine, giant arborvitae, lowland fir,

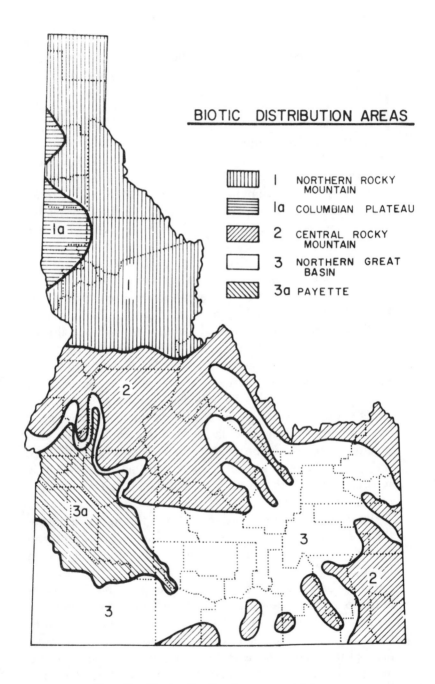

BIOTIC DISTRIBUTION AREAS

▥	1	NORTHERN ROCKY MOUNTAIN
▤	1a	COLUMBIAN PLATEAU
▨	2	CENTRAL ROCKY MOUNTAIN
☐	3	NORTHERN GREAT BASIN
▧	3a	PAYETTE

Fig. 7. Biotic distribution areas, Idaho

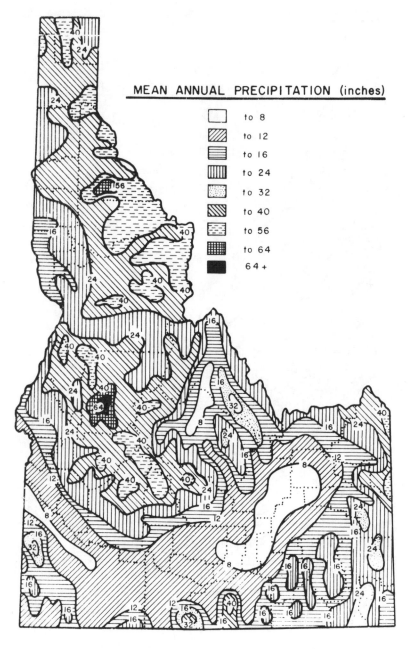

MEAN ANNUAL PRECIPITATION (inches)

	to 8
	to 12
	to 16
	to 24
	to 32
	to 40
	to 56
	to 64
	64 +

Fig. 8. Mean annual precipitation, Idaho.

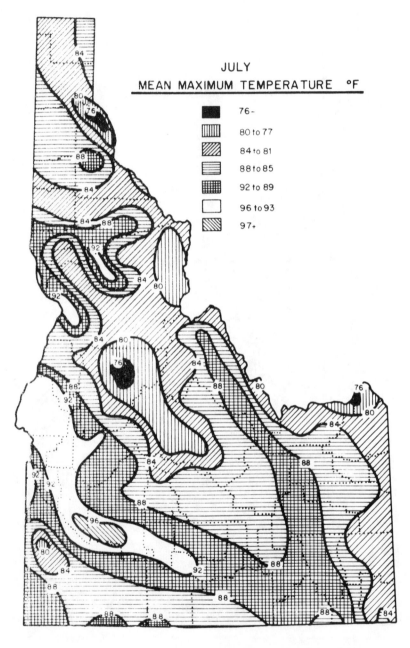

Fig. 9.   Mean maximum temperature (July), Idaho.

30

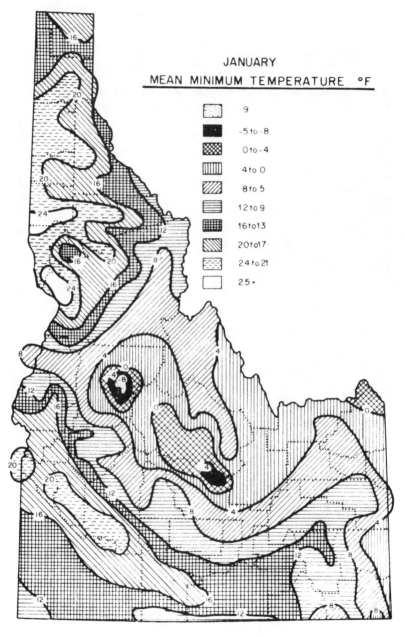

Fig. 10.   Mean minimum temperature (January), Idaho.

HORIZONTAL ZONATION OF VEGETATION

LOWEST TO HIGHEST ELEVATION:

    SEMI-ARID SAGEBRUSH AND PRAIRIE ZONES

    TIMBERED ZONE

    ALPINE ZONE

Fig. 11.   Horizontal zonation of vegetation, Idaho.

POPULATION DENSITIES
OF CULTURAL AREAS

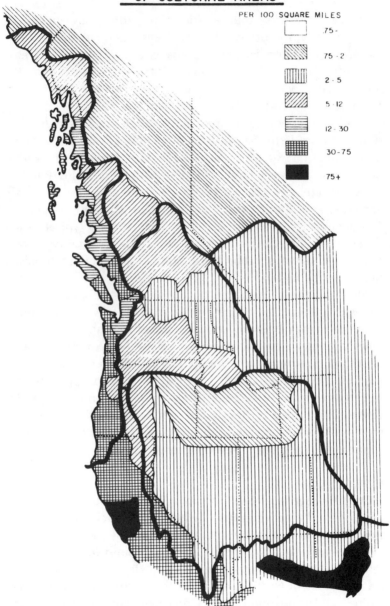

PER 100 SQUARE MILES

	.75 -
	75 - 2
	2 - 5
	5 - 12
	12 - 30
	30 - 75
	75+

Fig. 12. Population densities of cultural areas, northwestern
North America.

western hemlock, Douglas fir, yellow and lodgepole pine, Engelmann spruce, and alpine fir.

The central Rocky Mountain biotic area, zone 2, also includes numerous types of coniferous trees, particularly in its easternmost section. However, a smaller proportion of the area is forested due to lower annual rainfall (between 7 and 25 inches). Winters are longer and more severe here and temperature variations are greater than in zone 1.

Zone 3, the northern Great Basin biotic area, is radically different from both the northern and central Rocky Mountain biotic areas. In Idaho zone 3 is an undulating plain, with northern and eastern limits well defined by mountains. Rarely does the area receive more than 15 inches of precipitation annually, and about two-thirds of this precipitation is snow. Temperatures vary in the extreme. Vegetation is typical of a desert environment (Figure 11) and includes several types of sagebrush, salt sage, rabbit brush, juniper and, in the foothills, mountain mahogany.

Although these descriptions of Idaho's biotic areas are of necessity generalized and there are many local variations, the main point has been to show in broad outline the diverse environmental areas of Idaho and relate them to the distinct aboriginal cultures which emerged. Broad differences between the three biotic zones had an impact on Idaho's population distribution, as may be seen in Figure 12. The northern and central biotic areas obviously supported more people than the southern areas. Estimates for the average size of local groupings support this conclusion (see Chapter 3).

CONCLUSION

Over thousands of years the aboriginal inhabitants of Idaho developed distinctive cultures whose basic social institutions were in harmony with the natural environment. Archaeological research and the diversity of languages found in this region reflect the antiquity of this process. Idaho's location in two major cultural areas of North America — the Plateau and the Great Basin — and its proximity to the Great Plains culture area further reflect the diversity of its natural environment and cultures.

One gains the impression that in northern and central Idaho

subsistence was usually assured. A rich natural environment supported a denser population than in southern Idaho and usually provided a comfortable margin of survival. Thus, inhabitants could be selective in exploiting food resources. On the other hand, particularly before acquisition of the horse, the aboriginal inhabitants of southern Idaho were forced to move constantly as they exploited nearly all edible resources. Substantial local variations in temperature and rainfall produced varied flora and fauna, and a detailed knowledge of them was the key to survival in the south.

Fig. 13. V-shaped weir with cylinder basket trap.

CHAPTER 3

SUBSISTENCE

KUTENAI

The aboriginal Kutenai, extending into Montana and Canada (Figure 3), were divided into upper and lower divisions. Population density varied from 2 to 5 persons per 100 square miles and local groupings ranged from 100 to 200 individuals. Of course, these figures varied considerably according to the season and occasion. Linguistically the Kutenai were unrelated to any other group in the Plateau (Figures 4 and 5). The Upper Kutenai were more oriented toward the Great Plains culture area, and already had a well-developed horse complex by the time Euro-Americans arrived in the area.

The aboriginal territory of the Kutenai was rich in fish and game. Particularly, the Lower Kutenai harvested great quantities of fish including several types of salmon, white fish, trout, suckers, sturgeon, and squawfish. Throughout the year they hunted a number of large game animals found in their territory, including big horn sheep, Rocky Mountain goat, grizzly, brown, and black bear, moose, elk, white tail, black tail, and mule deer, and woodland caribou. Less important for subsistence were the coyote, lynx and wolf, although their furs were valued. Birds were also plentiful and the spruce grouse, ptarmigan, and several types of ducks, geese, and grouse constituted an important part of the diet.

This rich supply of fish, game and birds flourished in a well-watered environment. Not only was there abundant rainfall, but there was also substantial ground water replenished by the annual runoff from the mountains to the east. Generally, the area consisted of thickly forested slopes interspersed with well-watered, open valleys, which often contained small lakes and sloughs.

Annual temperature variations in aboriginal Kutenai territory were substantially less then in other parts of Idaho. The many

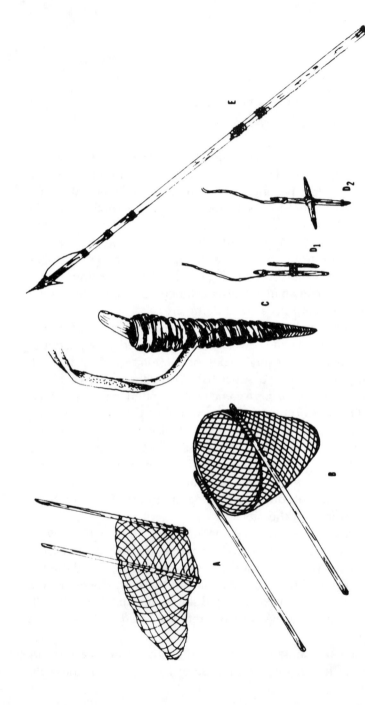

Fig. 14. Fishing implements: A and B — dip nets; C — harpoon head; D1 and D2 — hafted harpoon head on composite handle.

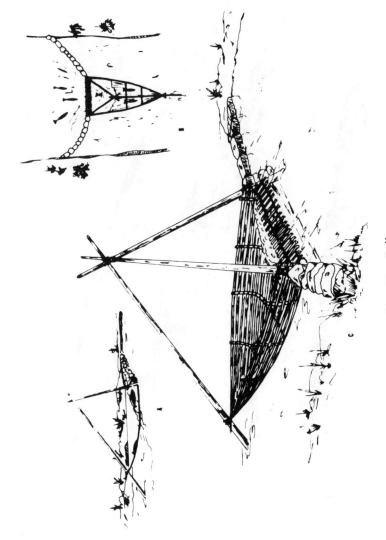

Fig. 15. Fall trap.

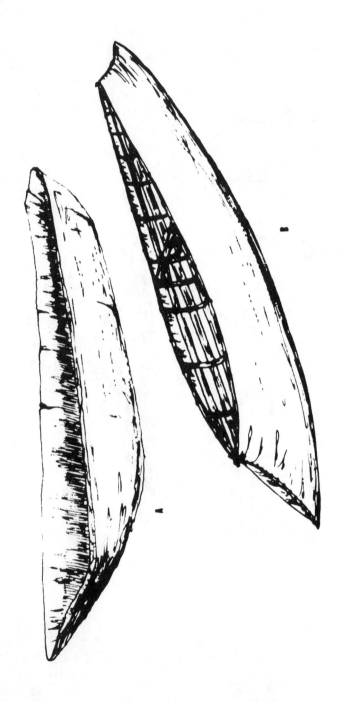

Fig. 16. Canoes: A — dugout canoe; B — bark-covered canoe.

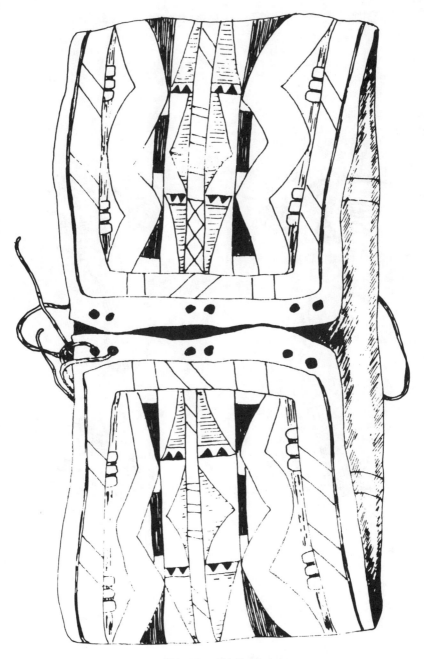

Fig. 17.   Parfleche.

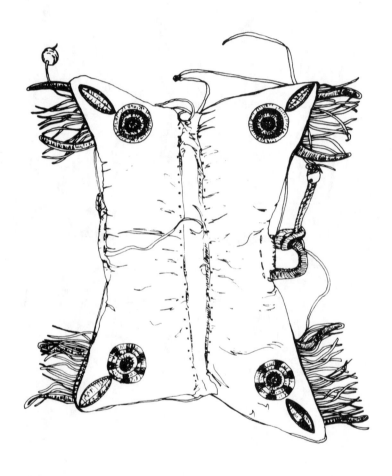

Fig. 18.   Man's saddle.

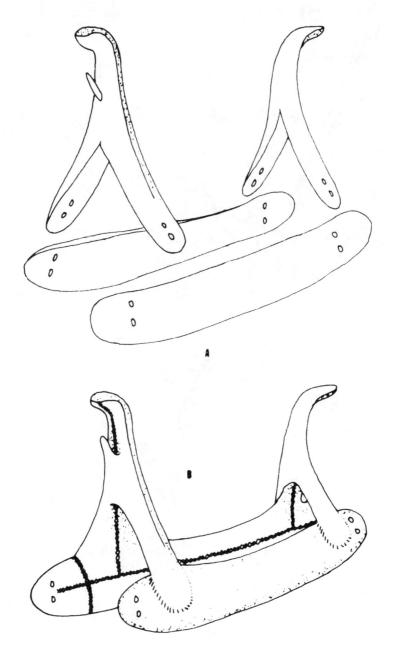

Fig. 19.   Woman's saddle.

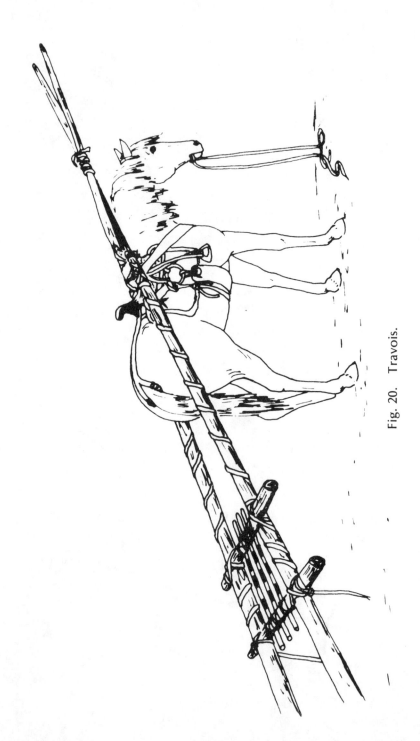

Fig. 20. Travois.

lakes and the Pacific Ocean had a moderating effect on the weather in this region producing a relatively mild climate. Rarely were there severe winters. Numerous food plants flourished here and were gathered by the Kutenai, including tuberous roots such as bitterroot, camas and wild onion. Also gathered were black moss, thornberries, huckleberries, serviceberries, blackberries, and chokecherries. Some nuts and seeds were eaten, although they were of lesser importance.

The annual cycle of subsistence activities began early in the spring among the Lower Kutenai with fishing for salmon and sturgeon, and somewhat later in June among the Upper Kutenai when they crossed over into the Great Plains to hunt bison. As the spring fishing season waned and the summer progressed, the women of both groups began gathering bitterroots and later camas as they moved into progressively higher elevations.

Generally the summer bison hunt of the Upper Kutenai lasted about four weeks, and when they returned from the Plains, they scattered to gather berries for the winter. Birds of various kinds were hunted during all seasons of the year.

When autumn began, the Lower Kutenai began communal deer drives, but the Upper Kutenai returned to the Great Plains to hunt bison once again. We are told that each family head expected to return with two or three pack horses laden with dried bison meat. Before the horse, dogs were used as pack animals for this chore. Both the Upper and Lower Kutenai cached their berries, dried meat, and roots in locations readily accessible to their winter settlements. Hunting and food gathering were curtailed during the winter months, but the Kutenai took some fish and occasional large game during the colder months.

Methods of taking and preserving birds, fish, and game were diverse. All varieties of fish were caught with devices such as cylinder baskets in v-shaped weirs, spears, and x-shaped gorges (Figures 13 and 14). Nets probably were not used. The Lower Kutenai excelled in the construction of fall traps (Figure 15) and possessed a generally superior set of fishing implements to those possessed by the Upper Kutenai. Bark-covered canoes were used by both groups (Figure 16). Fish were preserved by either sun-drying or drying over a fire, and stored in cedar boxes

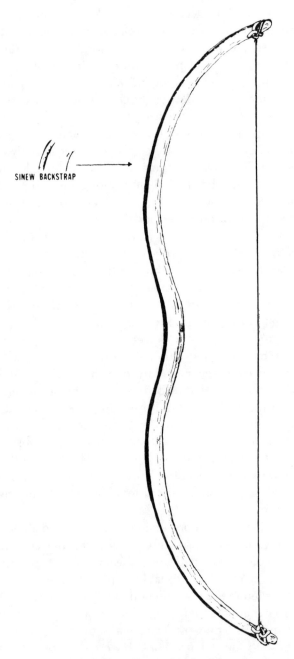

SINEW BACKSTRAP

Fig. 21.   Sinew-backed bow.

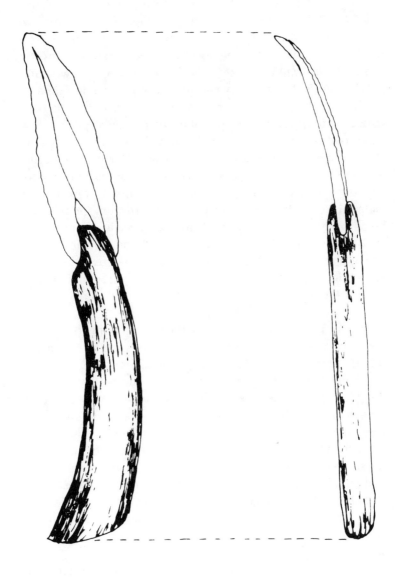

Fig. 22.   Mounted scraper.

(Lower Kutenai) or the parfleche (Upper Kutenai) (Figure 17). Fish were baked, boiled, or broiled, but we are told that boiling was the preferred method of cooking.

The Kutenai use of the horse closely resembled Plains practices. Both saddle and pack animals were used extensively, particularly by the Upper Kutenai who possessed more horses. Saddles were made from elkhorn frames covered by buckskin and were of three types: a man's saddle (Figure 18), a woman's saddle (Figure 19), and a pack saddle. Older people primarily used the riding saddles. The parfleche was used with pack saddles to transport many types of foods, particularly dried meat and roots, but the two pole drag, or travois, common among the Plains Indians (Figure 20), was not used. Horses were used, however, to drag lodge poles from place to place. Bridles, lariats, and other horse trappings were of rawhide, a very durable material. Young boys were the principal herdsmen and selective horse-breeding was practiced. Families normally owned from 3 to 5 horses per individual and the possession of many horses brought great social prestige. Poor people had few horses and less social prestige. Because of their social importance, horses were frequently traded, used as gifts, and were a major prize sought during raids on other groups.

Perhaps the most exciting use of the horse among the Kutenai was in hunting bison. A large circle of scouts was formed about one-quarter mile apart. After bison were sighted, scouts signaled the main body and began separating out the better animals in the herd, while others began shooting them in the shoulder or kidney area with bows made of wild cherry or cedar and reinforced with sinew (Figure 21). Rarely did any family head kill more than two bison per day because his wife could butcher and dry no more. The bison were skinned with knives made of stone and the hides were dressed with scrapers made from bison ribs and chipped stone (Figure 22). Most of the meat was dried, but small chunks were sometimes pulverized and mixed with wild peppermint before storage. Bison bones not used for tools were split for their marrow.

Among the Lower Kutenai, deer were a more important food source than bison and were hunted in communal drives directed by a deer hunting chief. Elk hides and mountain goat horns were

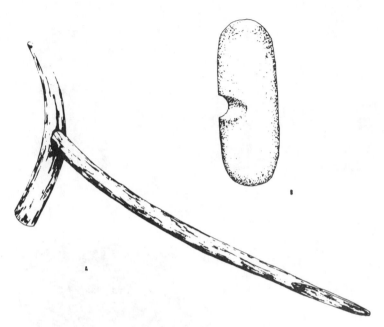

Fig. 23.   Digging stick with antler and stone handles.

especially prized by both groups, although these animals were hunted less frequently than bison or deer.

Women used two types of digging sticks to obtain roots, a willow stick with a fire-hardened point which was inserted into a deer horn handle, and a shorter stick made from the crotch of one prong of an elk horn (Figure 23). Each woman gathered as many roots as possible for her family each summer. Some roots were baked before storage, but others were sun-dried. During the winter months they were removed from storage, boiled in water with meat, and seasoned with pine moss, wild onions, and other condiments. Principal roots such as bitterroot and camas were cached in coiled, water-tight baskets (Figure 24) along with the highly prized serviceberries, huckleberries, and chokecherries. The Kutenai made a crude, sun-dried pottery but used mostly carved wooden bowls and horn spoons for eating.

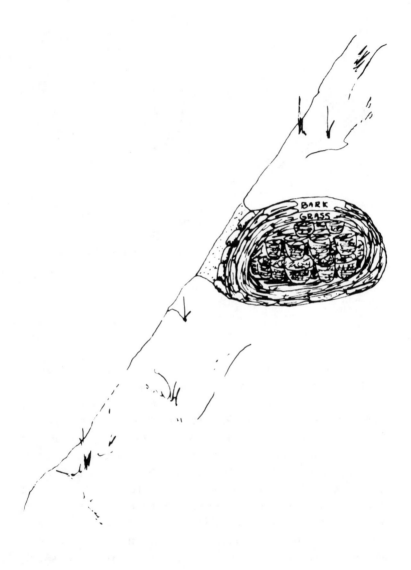

Fig. 24.   Cache pit with storage baskets.

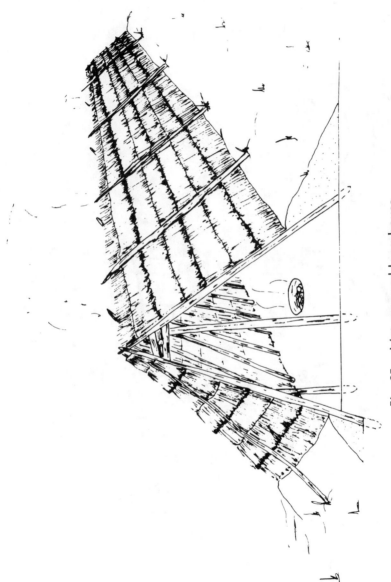

Fig. 25.   Mat-covered long-house.

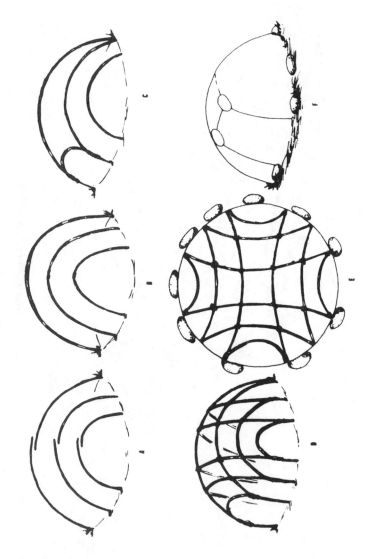

Fig. 26. Sweat house construction.

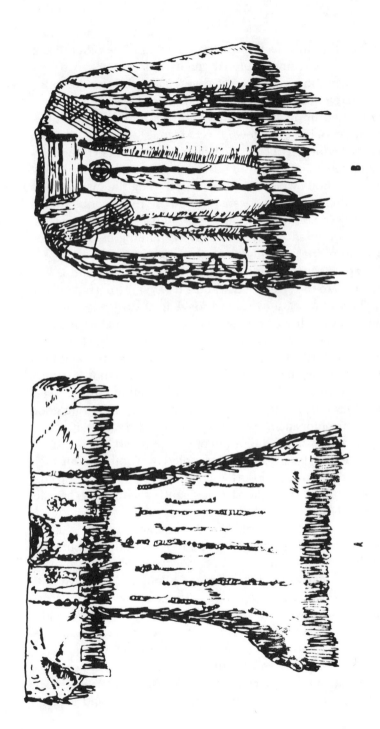

Fig. 27. Clothing: A — woman's buckskin dress; B — man's buckskin shirt.

Before the introduction of the horse and intensified Plains influence, the Upper Kutenai spent their winters in typical Plateau semisubterranean, mat-covered long-houses. Although these were not as large as some found elsewhere in the Plateau, they housed up to fifty people with room for as many as five separate cooking fires down the center aisle (Figure 25). Soon after they adopted horses, the Upper Kutenai began using skin-covered tents similar to those used by tribes of the Great Plains. However, the Lower Kutenai were still using the mat-covered house when Euro-Americans arrived in the region. In the summer both Lower and Upper Kutenai used the isolated conical tipi when family groups were hunting and gathering roots and berries in outlying resource areas.

Other structures found among both the Upper and Lower Kutenai were the sweat house and a bark menstrual hut (Figure 26). The sweat house was used for religious, recreational and health reasons. It was a small, hemispherical structure made of flexible saplings covered with mats. Steam and heat came from stones which were heated outside over an open fire and then moved into a small rock-lined pit inside the sweat house, where they were sprinkled with water. Regular bathing in the sweat house was thought to produce strong bodies and bring good luck. Both minor and major illnesses were also treated with sweat bathing and associated dips in cold streams and lakes. The less elaborate menstrual huts were occupied by women during their menstrual periods and during childbirth. It was believed that women should be isolated from contact with most people, particularly men, at these times.

Men's clothing among the Upper and Lower Kutenai resembled Plains Indian clothing and consisted of a buckskin shirt, leggings, breech cloth, and moccasins. Shirts were made from two hides with a full collar and a long neck (Figure 27B). Women wore an undecorated fringed Plains skin frock supplemented by a soft, knee-length legging during the colder months. Hats were made from rawhide, fur, and willow withes, and distinguished warriors decorated their heads with feathers. Warriors among the Lower Kutenai wore a slat body armor for defense against the war clubs, arrows, spears, and knives used by their enemies. Footware consisted of moccasins and leggings which were worn when needed.

The Upper and Lower Kutenai divided their food in different ways. We are told that among the Upper Kutenai a man owned the meat of any animal he killed, whereas the Lower Kutenai usually gave their kill to a hunting leader who distributed it. Fish traps were individually owned among the Upper Kutenai, but the Lower Kutenai built and owned their traps communally, taking directions from a fishing leader who divided the catch among all members of the community. Patterns of ownership give the impression that the Upper Kutenai were more individualistic, perhaps in keeping with their Plains orientation.

KALISPEL

Aboriginally, the Kalispel occupied a vast territory south of the Kutenai extending into Montana, Washington, and Canada (Figure 3), and were closely related to the Coeur d'Alene and other Interior Salishans (Figures 4 and 5). Their population density probably ranged from 2 to 5 persons per 100 square miles (Figure 12), and local groups rarely exceeded 100 individuals, although seasonal and ceremonial variation was substantial. They lived in a natural environment quite similar to that of the Kutenai — heavily forested, mountainous, well-watered, and with many green meadows. Temperature and precipitation patterns were similar to those described for Kutenai territory, except that lakes were not as numerous.

In general, the same birds and game available to the aboriginal Kutenai were available to the Kalispel. Because they had no salmon runs in their territory, they often traveled into neighboring British Columbia to fish. They also fished and traded with the Spokane and other Interior Salishans to the west at Kettle Falls and Spokane Falls. Fish taken in their territory included trout, whitefish, squawfish, and suckers.

Large game animals hunted included elk, moose, deer, mountain goat, mountain sheep, brown bear, and grizzly bear. Bison and possibly antelope were hunted in the Great Plains and even caribou were occasionally hunted. Numerous small game animals such as rabbit and beaver and birds such as ducks and geese added to this abundant set of resources. Two major root crops, the bitterroot and camas, provided a large portion of the daily diet. Numerous berries and nuts were relished, including raspberries, thimbleberries, blackberries, red and black gooseberries, blueberries, chokecherries, currants, hazelnuts, and at least two types of pine nuts.

In spring and early summer the Kalispel began fishing on Lake Pend d'Oreille and digging for early roots. Root digging continued into midsummer, particularly in large meadows around Cusick, Washington, where they were joined by the Spokane and Colville. In August, Kalispel bison hunting parties left for Montana, usually going up the Clark Fork along the Pend d'Oreille trail. The men resumed fishing in the late summer and early fall at which time berries were also gathered and stored by the women. October saw the most intensive hunting for deer, as all members of the community labored to amass adequate food for subsistence during the winter months of November, December, and January, which were spent mostly in winter villages. When stored foods ran low during the winter, some hunting was undertaken in the river valleys to replenish supplies, but winter was mostly devoted to ceremonial activity and handicrafts.

Women gathered most of the roots and berries and men concentrated on fishing and hunting. Most subsistence labor was done in groups. Men usually fished with dip nets, hook and line, spears, weirs, and traps (Figures, 13, 14 and 15). Bark-covered canoes with frames of cedar aided them particularly in lake fishing. Fish were also dried and stored for winter subsistence. Deer and elk were hunted cooperatively in a slowly constricting circle of hunters, sometimes several miles in circumference, and generally were killed with spears and arrows. Horses were sometimes used to help drive large game animals into lakes and other natural traps where they were speared and clubbed. A variant of this method was the forced drive of game through narrow passages where the animals could be easily shot. There is some evidence that the Kalispel used rattlesnake poison to tip their arrows for certain game and drove game over cliffs. Some stories describe how outstanding hunters would run down game in thick brush or in deep snow by snow shoe. Fire was used to smoke out hibernating bears and to drive game into prearranged traps. Before acquiring the horse, the

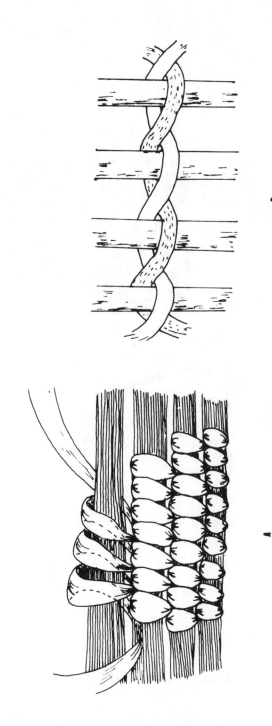

Fig. 28. Basketry: A — coiled basketry; B — twined basketry.

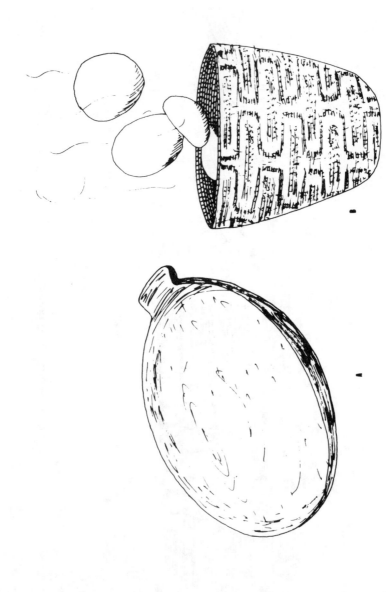

Fig. 29. Implements: A — wooden seed parching tray; B — stone boiling in water-filled basket.

Kalispel may have hunted bison on foot by ambush at water holes and by picking off stragglers from the main herd.

Only limited numbers of horses have been reported for the Kalispel; the thick forests in their territory made large herds of horses impractical. Like the Kutenai, Kalispel use of the horse closely resembled uses of the horse in the Great Plains. As with northern Idaho, they probably received horses from the south, but apparently did not come to rely on them as much as the Upper Kutenai described above. One estimate lists the Kalispel as averaging about 1 to 2 horses per person; this may be an exaggeration.

The tools of the Kalispel closely resembled Kutenai tools. They used coiled basketry of various shapes (Figure 28A) and rawhide containers, both watertight. As elsewhere in Idaho, food was sometimes cooked by dropping heated stones into these water-filled baskets (Figure 29B). Spoons were made of mountain sheep horn and imported moose and bison horn (Figure 30B); wooden spoons and bowls were also common. Stone pestles were used with various kinds of mortars to grind roots, meat, berries, and other foods. Earth ovens were in common use for roots, but meat was usually barbecued over open fires. Very durable crutch-handled digging sticks, painted on both ends, were made of iron wood and yew; splitting wedges were made of deer and elk horn. Arrow tips, spear points, knives, and pipes were made of various types of stone, and the double-curved bow was preferred. Syringa was regarded as the best kind of wood for these bows which were usually reinforced with sinew.

A few elderly Kalispel informants have described a semisubterranean lodge, which was probably out of use by the time Euro-Americans arrived in the area. Long lodges of double lean-to construction were used in the winter villages. In larger villages there were at least two such structures used as dwellings, one also used by the elders and leading men for meetings and the other by the community for ceremonial and festive affairs. Mat-covered, conical lodges holding two or more families were in common use during the warmer months but, as among the Kutenai, a skin cover rapidly replaced the mat cover when the Kalispel began using the horse to hunt bison in the Great Plains. Some elderly Kalispel have described a double lean-to, bark-

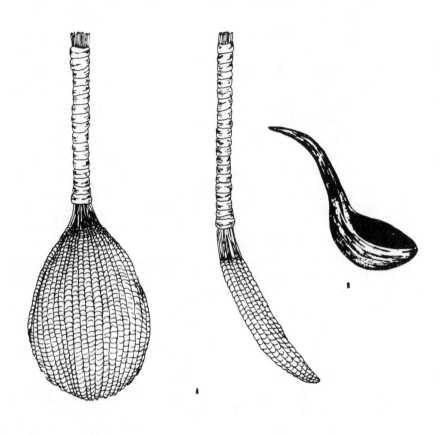

Fig. 30. Cooking implements: A — basketry ladle;
B — horn spoon.

Fig. 31.   Plains-type feathered headdress.

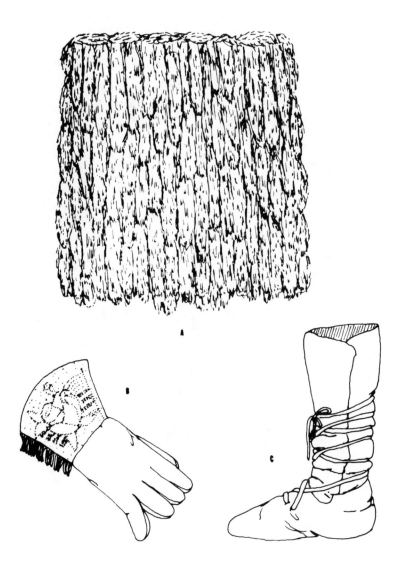

Fig. 32. Clothing: A — rabbit skin robe; B — buckskin glove;
C — high top moccasin.

covered lodge used in prehorse times, and a simple brush hut used in temporary hunting or gathering locations. The Kalispel may also have used an elevated platform structure for storage. Both the sweat house with a mat cover and a separate menstrual hut for women were in use.

Kalispel clothing conformed closely to styles of the Great Plains groups. Men wore a long, fringed buckskin shirt reaching to the hips with long leggings, breech cloths, belts, moccasins (two types), and either hats or head bands. Sometimes long aprons were added. In the winter, moccasins were stuffed with fur for warmth and caps of fur were worn. Scalps were sometimes attached to a special shirt called a war shirt and, in recent times, feathered bonnets were adopted by some Kalispel (Figure 31). Women wore long dresses reaching to the ankles, short leggings, belts, headbands or caps, and moccasins. Dresses usually were made of two deer or small elk skins fastened face-to-face. Their clothing was decorated by fringing, pinking, puncturing, painting, and burning in designs. Quills, beads, elk teeth, shells, and ermine fur were also added. Prized robes of bison skin were tanned with the hair on, and robes (Figure 32A), skin ponchos, and mittens were made of rabbit fur. Some men and women decorated their skin with tattoos.

COEUR D'ALENE

Aboriginal Coeur d'Alene territory encompassed approximately four million acres and extended into Montana and Washington (Figure 3). Population density is estimated to have ranged from 2 to 5 persons per 100 square miles (Figure 12), and local groups ranged from 100 to 200 persons with seasonal and ceremonial variations. Coeur d'Alene territory centered on present Lake Coeur d'Alene and in general resembled that of the Kutenai and Kalispel, except that the extreme western portion of the territory was flat, open grassland well suited for grazing. The relatively high mountainous region of their eastern boundary assured a substantial annual precipitation (Figure 8) which fed their many lakes and streams. Like the Kalispel, the Coeur d'Alene spoke an Interior Salishan language closely related to Spokane (Figures 4 and 5).

The Coeur d'Alene hunted deer, elk, and bear, and, like their

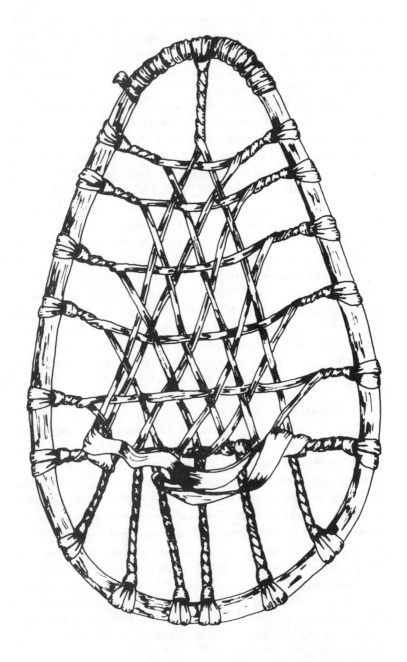

Fig. 33. Snow shoe.

neighbors to the north and south, crossed into the western Great Plains of Montana to hunt bison. Small game included beaver, marmot, squirrel, badger, and rabbit. Because streams in their territory contained few fish, the Coeur d'Alene traveled south to the North Fork of the Clearwater River and west to Spokane Falls and Kettle Falls where they fished with the Nez Perces, Colville, Spokane and other tribes. Fish taken in their own territory included white fish, trout, squawfish, and we are told that mussels and snails were also eaten. The camas root was unusually abundant and a large surplus was gathered for trade. Bitterroot and wild onion were of secondary importance, but still widely used. The Coeur d'Alene also consumed many berries, nuts, and other delicacies such as wild rhubarb.

In the spring, fishing began with some groups traveling to neighboring tribal areas to the south and west to intercept the early salmon runs, while others stayed at home to gather locally available spring foods. Fishing implements included the hook and line, spears, harpoons, weirs, traps, dip nets, and prepared dipping platforms. We are told that a fishing specialist or leader regulated construction and use of the large weirs and traps, and that he could magically entice fish into them. The root harvest began in June with small groups moving from one area to another to gather the roots as they ripened. During June and July large groups gathered to dig camas in three major locations — the area just south of present Desmet, Idaho; the area around present Clarkia, Idaho; and the area around Moscow, Idaho. These three areas were also centers for ceremonies and trading, and intertribal groups formed at these locations for joint bison hunting ventures into the Great Plains during the late summer months.

In early fall white fish were taken in Coeur d'Alene territory and many berries and nuts were stored for the winter. During the winter months there was only a limited amount of fishing and hunting. Snow shoes (Figure 33) and, later, horses were used to run down the game as among the Kalispel and other tribes of the Plateau.

Underbrush in the forested areas was burned off periodically to facilitate hunting and promote growth of browse for deer and elk. Areas with large big game populations were encircled with

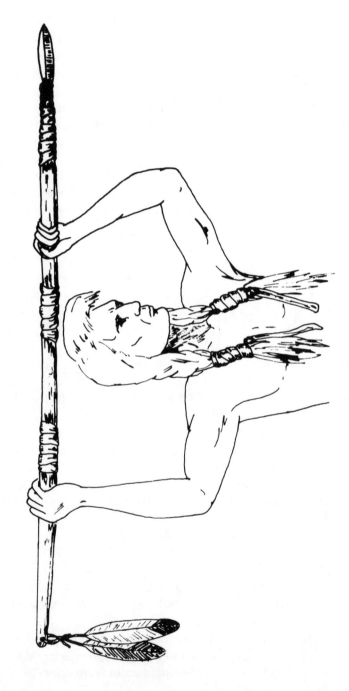

Fig. 34. Man with war spear.

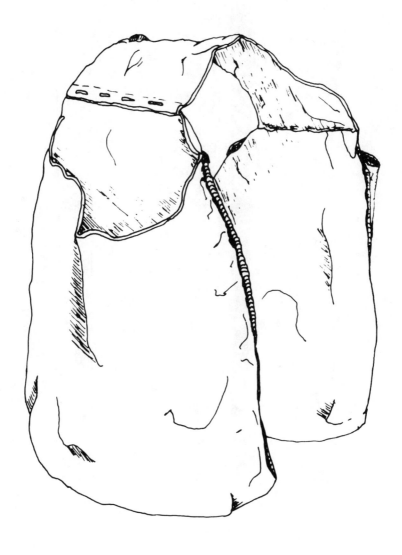

Fig. 35.   Saddle bags.

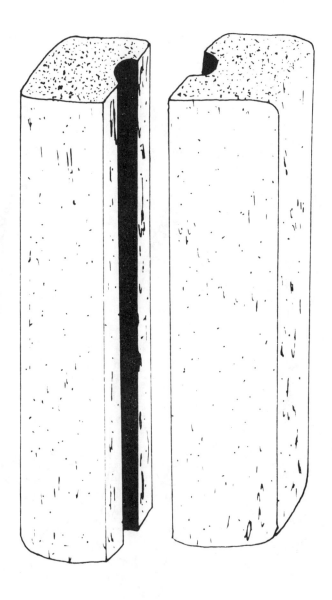

Fig. 36. Sandstone shaft sander.

concentric rings of fire until the animals were trapped in a small central area. Hunting specialists directed these communal hunts which also included chasing the game into lakes where it was killed from canoes. Another method of encirclement depended on the use of *scarecrows*. Pieces of human clothing were tied on trees and brush in a large semicircle. Men under the direction of a hunting specialist then closed the circle, driving the animals toward the scarecrows where they stopped and were easily killed with spears and other weapons (Figure 34). Such communal techniques produced kills as large as 400 deer in recorded cases. Communal deer hunts were sometimes conducted during the winter in areas of lower elevation.

The relatively few horses possessed by the Coeur d'Alene were used in communal hunts and on trips to distant root digging and fishing stations. In general, Coeur d'Alene horse culture resembled the practices described above for the Upper Kutenai with only minor variations. Bridles were made of hair. Two men's saddles were in use, one built on a wooden base covered by rawhide and another on a pad of deer fur covered with leather. The familiar travois was rarely used because the forested Coeur d'Alene territory was better suited to packing (Figure 35). Selective horse-breeding was practiced and small herds were kept mostly on the rolling grassland in western Coeur d'Alene territory. As with most tribes in the Great Plains and eastern Plateau, boys were the principal herders. The best source available estimates that there were from 2 to 3 horses per individual. Richer families possessed more horses, and the Coeur d'Alene living in the western, more open portion of the territory, possessed more horses than those living in the hilly, wooded portions to the east and north.

The basic materials for most Coeur d'Alene tools were bone, antler, stone, wood, and sinew. Bows were made of syringa backed with sinew, and arrows were tipped with stone. Easily flaked stone was used to make many piercing and cutting implements, but sandstone was used for grinding, sharpening and polishing implements (Figure 36). Hammers and pestles were made mostly from river cobbles. Horn spoons were carved and shaped by steaming on wooden molds, whereas other spoons and pestles were made of wood. Decorative dyes were made from minerals and vegetables and used on buckskin clothing, which was sewn with bear bone needles and threads of sinew and vegetable fiber. The woman's essential digging stick, made primarily from syringa, was curved with a crutch handle. Although no evidence exists for sun-dried pottery among the Coeur d'Alene, they did make storage boxes from bark, hide, and woven hemp. Food was cooked in earth ovens and by the familiar methods of stone boiling in woven and coiled baskets and bark containers. Meat was broiled on an open fire while suspended on hemispherically-shaped spits or inclined sticks stuck in the ground. Earth ovens were used for cooking large amounts of meat and most types of roots that were not dried in the sun.

The Coeur d'Alene used both the mat-covered, double lean-to, long-house and the conical lodge. Long-houses regularly included ten or more families and were the scene of large ceremonies, especially during winter months. Typical Plateau sweat houses and menstrual huts described above were found in most Coeur d'Alene settlements. Elevated storage platforms with mat or bark covering and ladders were widely used and it is said that some Coeur d'Alene villages had circular stockades of posts for defensive purposes. Occasionally, long-houses were also fortified with extra earth and logs on their roofs.

Both men and women wore buckskin tunics with long, loose sleeves which reached to the men's knees and the women's ankles. In winter, men wore leggings and fringed robes of bison, deer, and elk hide. Robes were also made from small animal furs including marmot, ground squirrel, beaver, coyote, lynx, and probably rabbit.

NEZ PERCES

Estimates of aboriginal Nez Perce territory range as high as 27,000 square miles. They probably were the largest group in aboriginal Idaho with a population density of 5 to 12 persons per 100 square miles (Figure 12), with local groups normally ranging from 30 to 200 individuals, depending on the season and the type of social grouping. Some anthropologists have divided them into the Upper and Lower Nez Perces, primarily on a basis of language differences. The Upper Nez Perces, like the Upper

Kutenai, were more oriented toward a Great Plains life style. The Nez Perces are also closely related linguistically to the Sahaptian speakers of Oregon and Washington, such as the Yakima and Umatilla (Figures 4 and 5). A substantial portion of their central territory was in the Columbian Plateau biotic subarea (Figure 7) which was particularly well suited to raising horses. The Nez Perces and their adjoining western neighbors, the Cayuse, possessed the largest herds of horses found anywhere in the Great Basin, Plateau, or Northwest Coast culture areas.

Nez Perce territory spanned the Clearwater River and the northern portion of the Salmon River drainage basins (Figure 2). It was marked by a great diversity of flora, fauna, temperature and precipitation patterns caused primarily by sharp differences in elevation. It was a more varied natural environment than we have seen in the territories of the Kutenai, Kalispel, or Coeur d'Alene. The deep canyons cut by the Clearwater, Salmon, and Snake rivers brought about extensive seasonal migrations for food. The various roots exploited by the Nez Perces ripened early in the spring in the lower elevations of the Lewiston area, but roots in areas such as Weippe sometimes did not ripen until mid-August. The basic root staple was camas, but bitterroot, kouse, wild carrot, and wild onion were also important. Fruits gathered included serviceberries, gooseberries, hawthornberries, thornberries, huckleberries, currants, and chokecherries. Pine nuts, sunflower seeds, and black moss added to these abundant vegetable and fruit resources.

The Nez Perces were the most renowned horsemen of aboriginal Idaho and used their horses in most subsistence activities. Men, women and children were all mounted on the annual and seasonal movements back and forth between the various resource areas. Relative wealth in horses was the major distinguishing factor between the upper and lower classes. Well-known leaders and their families commonly had large herds; some families are said to have owned several hundred horses. One estimate states there were from 5 to 7 horses per individual. The Nez Perces had elaborate horse trappings made of rawhide, horse hair, bone, and antler and decorated with dyes, porcupine quills, and beads. Different saddles were made for men and women and for packing. The travois was used widely to transport heavy equipment, the idea apparently being adopted from the former dog travois. In fact, the dog and the horse have practically the same name in the Nez Perce language. The Nez Perces practiced selective horse-breeding, and boys were the principal herders. Although they bred for strength and endurance, the Nez Perces did not breed for particular colors as did the Euro-Americans with the present-day Appaloosa. Horses were exchanged as gifts, sold, and acquired through raids.

Large game animals hunted in aboriginal Nez Perce territory included the elk, deer, moose, mountain sheep and goat, as well as black, brown, and grizzly bear. After they obtained the horse, many Nez Perces made annual trips to Montana to secure bison and antelope. Occasionally, small game animals were caught when needed, including rabbit, squirrel, badger, and marmot. Birds taken were ducks, geese, grouse, and sage hens. The aboriginal Nez Perces were particularly fortunate to have a large number of anadromous fish and many streams well suited for exploitation. The Nez Perces took the chinook, silver, dog, and blueback varieties of salmon; dolly varden, cutthroat, lake, and steelhead varieties of trout; several kinds of suckers; white fish; sturgeon; lampreys; and squawfish. A recent study estimates their average, annual per capita consumption of fish as over 400 pounds.

In the early spring when the cache pits had been emptied of stored food, the Nez Perces began communal drives in the river valleys, snow shoe hunting, and trips down the Snake and Columbia rivers to intercept the early salmon runs. This was facilitated by the horse, which enabled the Nez Perces to visit most parts of the Northwest and the Plains on a regular basis. Before this they traveled widely by canoe and used dogs as pack animals. As the spring progressed, salmon began arriving in Nez Perce territory, and the early root crop was taken in the lower territory. Although hunting was more or less continuous, it was of lesser importance during the salmon runs when all the able-bodied men turned to fishing.

By midsummer the Nez Perces were leaving their villages in the river valleys and moving into the highlands where later-growing crops were harvested, highland streams were fished, and hunting became more intense. The fall salmon runs and hunting provided winter food stores. Brief bison hunting trips into Montana through passes such as the Lolo Trail took place in late summer to augment winter supplies. These large hunting parties often included members of neighboring tribes and were led by famous warriors. Some Nez Perce parties stayed in the Plains for several years at a time, and few winters passed that did not see some wintering with the Flathead in Montana. By November most travel had ceased and the Nez Perces were settled in their winter villages until the cycle began again in the early spring.

Men were the principal fishermen, although women assisted in splitting, drying, and storing the salmon. Hook and line, spears, harpoons, dip nets, traps, and weirs (Figure 37) were used. Traps and weirs often were constructed communally by villages and regulated by a fishing specialist who divided the catch (Figure 38). Sometimes the weirs and traps were close to winter villages, but often they were up from the major tributaries on smaller streams. Salmon were dipped from dugout canoes and dipping platforms on the major tributaries (Figure 39). Fish were sun-dried and smoked for winter storage.

Deer and elk were taken communally by encirclement methods similar to those used by the Coeur d'Alene. Decoys, scarecrows, and similar devices were used to entice them into areas where they could be shot easily. Fire and horses were also used to drive deer and elk into traps. A variant of the lake entrapment used by the Coeur d'Alene was to drive deer and elk into the large tributaries where they could be easily dispatched from canoes and horseback. The ambush was a popular method particularly in prehorse days when it was used for bison in Montana. Deadfalls were popular for larger game as were snares for birds and smaller game (Figure 40). Some evidence exists for the use of rattlesnake poison on arrow tips.

Women dug roots with crutch-handled digging sticks. Sun-dried pottery was made but coiled basketry was the major form of container (Figure 41). Food was stored in baskets in bark and grass-lined cache pits usually found on well-drained hillsides. Some horn spoons and drinking cups were made, but most spoons and bowls were wooden. Stone pestles were used with both basketry (with a stone base) and wooden mortars (Figure

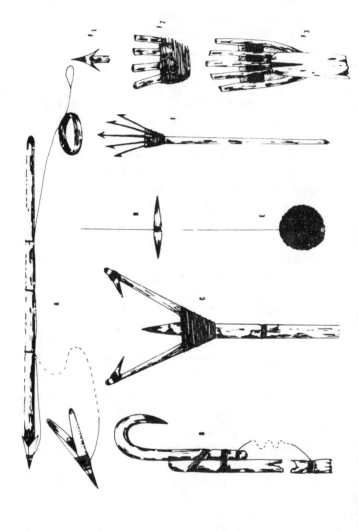

Fig. 37. Fishing implements: A — mounted harpoon with retrieval line; B — mounted detachable gaff hook with retrieval line; C — leister; D — bone gorge; E — horse hair sniggle; F — gig and elements of construction.

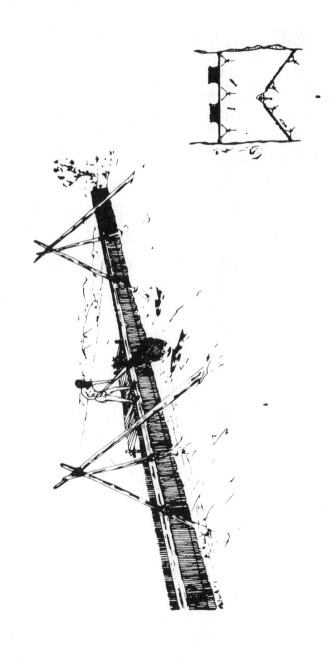

Fig. 38. Weirs: A — weir with dipping platform; view of upstream and downstream portions of weir.

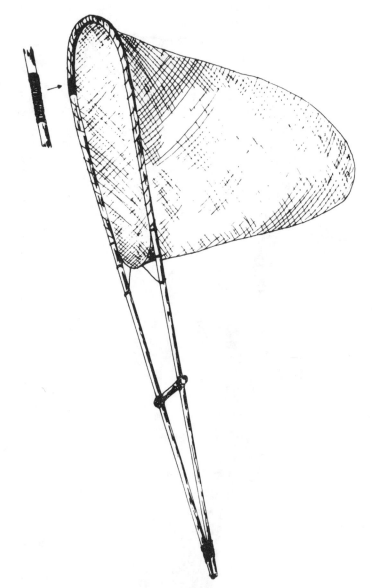

Fig. 39.   Short handled dip net.

Fig. 40. Deadfalls: A — rock deadfall with construction; B — log deadfall with construction.

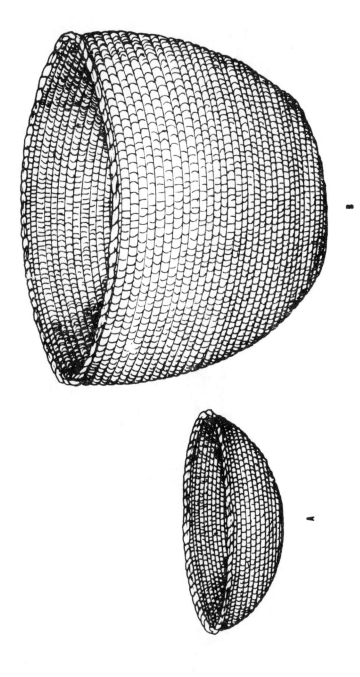

Fig. 41. Baskets: A — utilitarian domestic basket; B — storage basket.

42), primarily to grind meat and roots. Splitting wedges were made of antler, and clubs and axes were of stone; the latter were hafted with a combination of antler and wood. Bows were of syringa and yew and, like those of the Kutenai, Kalispel and Coeur d'Alene, backed with sinew. Roots and meats were boiled in baskets by the stone boiling method and baked in large earthen ovens. Generally, meat was broiled by attaching it to a wooden frame or sticks inserted in the ground around an open fire (Figure 43). Roots were crushed and formed into loaves and fist biscuits for storage.

The principal aboriginal Nez Perce house was the mat-covered, double lean-to long-house found generally among Plateau groups. It could be quite large, measuring well over a hundred feet in length. Normally, such large ones were temporary structures used on ceremonial occasions. Isolated conical tents (Figure 44) were used on the trail and when hunting, fishing, or root digging in temporary locations. Mat covers were gradually replaced by bison skin covers (Figure 45). Strong evidence exists for shallow semisubterranean men's and women's dormitories which were also used for sweat bathing (Figure 46). The typical, hemispherical, Plateau sweat house also was found in Nez Perce settlements as were the menstrual hut and submerged hot bath (Figure 49).

Aboriginal Nez Perce clothing was of the northern Plains type. Long, fringed buckskin shirts, leggings, belts, breech cloths, and several types of moccasins and gloves were worn by men (Figure 47). Feathered bonnets borrowed from the Plains were popular by the time Euro-Americans arrived in the area. Nez Perce men also wore robes of several types, particularly bison skin robes. However, most of their buckskin clothing was made from deer and elk hides. Women wore long, belted buckskin dresses, basketry caps (Figures 47 and 48), and knee-length moccasins. Both sexes used face painting for various purposes, and women decorated their dresses with elk teeth. Decorations also were made from vegetable and mineral dyes, porcupine quills, and many kinds of shell and bone beads. Furs were worn by women in their braids and sometimes fringed on their clothes.

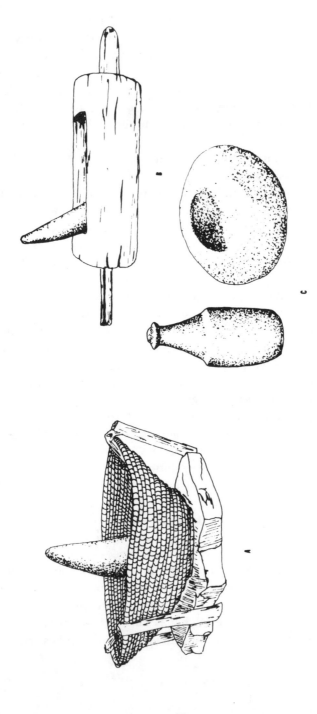

Fig. 42. Mortars: A — basket mortar with stone pestle and base; B — wooden mortar with stone pestle; C — stone mortar and pestle.

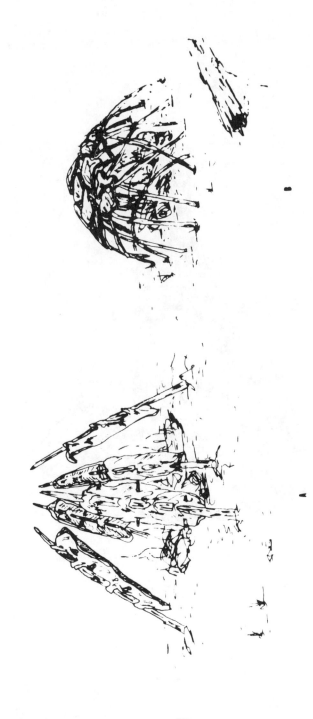

Fig. 43. Cooking techniques: A — meat broiling technique; B — meat drying and smoking techniques.

Fig. 44.   Mat-covered conical dwelling.

Fig. 45.　Skin-covered conical dwelling.

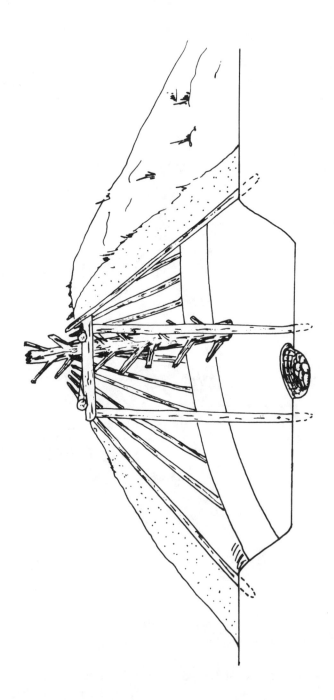

Fig. 46. Semisubterranean dormitory.

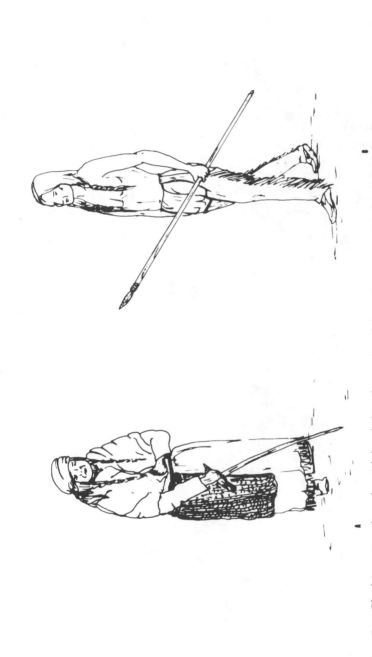

Fig. 47. Clothing: A — female with buckskin dress, shawl, hat, digging stick, and collecting bag; B — male with breech cloth, high leggings, low moccasins, and hunting spear.

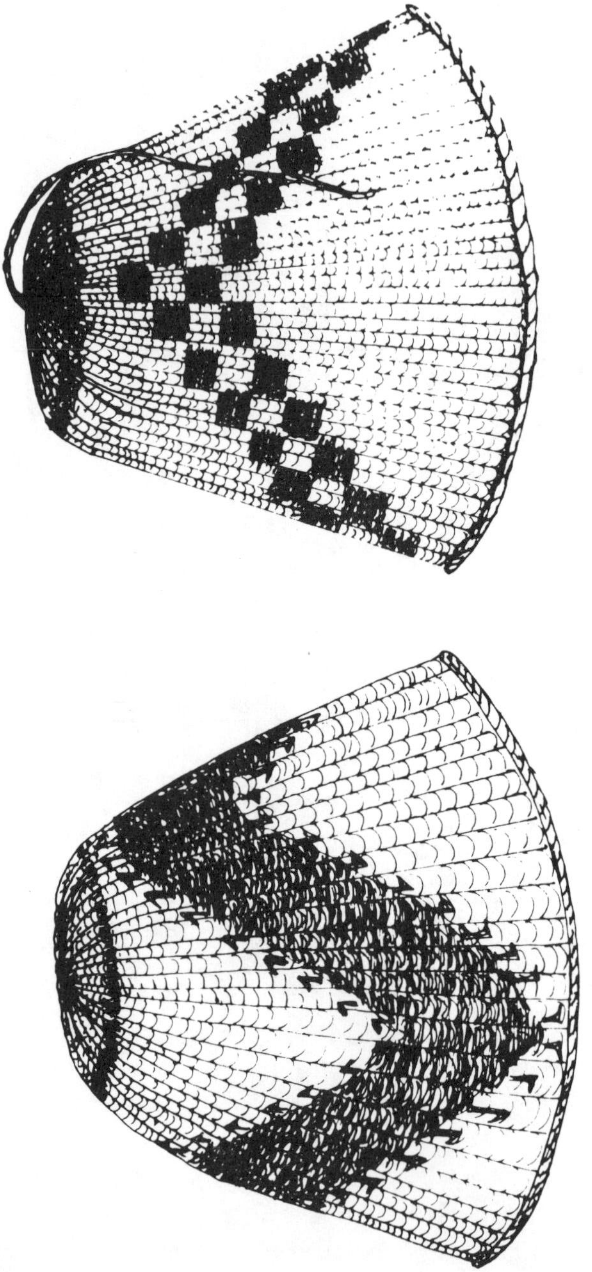

Fig. 48. Women's basketry hats.

SHOSHONE-BANNOCK

By now the reader will have noted the great similarities in subsistence among the aboriginal cultures of northern and central Idaho. The Kutenai, Kalispel, Coeur d'Alene, and Nez Perces shared a broadly similar environment with a healthy margin of survival (Figures 7, 8, 9 and 10). Their foods, tools, housing, and clothing were remarkably similar. Although influenced by Plains culture traits because of their easterly position in the Plateau culture area, they all shared the basic cultural patterns of the Plateau.

The aboriginal inhabitants of the northern Great Basin culture area followed a very distinctive way of life. They lived in an environment of comparatively low subsistence potential with very sparse population, and their economic patterns exemplify these facts quite clearly. The Shoshone-Bannock included two linguistically distinct groups — the Northern, or so-called Snake River Shoshone, and the Bannock. The Snake River Shoshone were divided into a number of bands such as the well-known Lemhi Shoshone. The Bannock minority were a small intrusive group who spoke a dialect of the Northern Paiute language (Figures 4 and 5). There is some evidence that until recently the Bannock were located farther west as part of the widespread Northern Paiute of Oregon, Nevada, and the eastern portion of modern California (Figure 3). Although occasionally acting independently, their common possession of the horse and exploitation of the same natural environment had produced similar social institutions among the Shoshone and Bannock by the time Euro-Americans moved into the region. Therefore, it is logical to lump the aboriginal Shoshone-Bannock into a single culture for purposes of general description. The aboriginal population density of this composite group ranged from 1.5 to 2 persons per 100 square miles (Figure 12). In prehorse days local groups rarely reached 100 individuals.

The aboriginal territory of the Shoshone-Bannock extended across most of southern Idaho into western Wyoming and well down into Nevada and Utah. This area rarely received more than 15 inches of precipitation annually, and many areas went for years without recorded rainfall. However, the higher elevations on the northern and eastern peripheries of their territory received

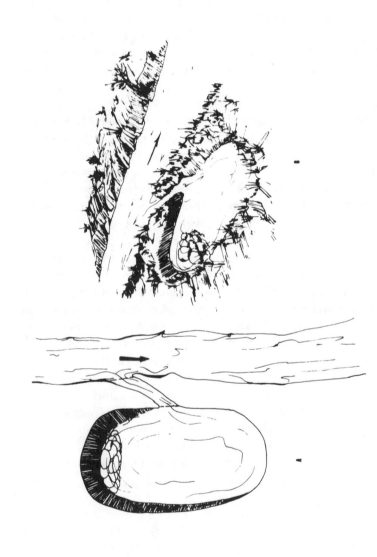

Fig. 49. Hot baths: A — submerged hot bath, overhead view; B — the same, side view.

greater annual precipitation. Here vegetation and animal life were more abundant. Similarly, the presence of the Snake River running across southern Idaho added to the area's capacity to support human life.

The Shoshone-Bannock, as well as their neighbors the Northern Paiute in southwestern Idaho, regularly took salmon below Snoshone Falls. Roots were more abundant here, particularly around present Weiser. In the prehorse period and more recently among the horseless groups of Shoshone-Bannock, there was an important reliance on small game, birds, insects, seeds, and nuts. They closely resembled the Northern Paiute in this respect. Groundhog, jack rabbit, cottontail, porcupine, prairie dog, rodents, and badger were important sources of meat. Grasshoppers, crickets, ants, and larvae of various insects also were regularly taken, and bird eggs were collected occasionally. It has been reported that some inhabitants of this region exploited well over 100 different types of seed plants. Acquisition of the horse probably decreased Shoshone-Bannock dependence on small game and plants. Those with horses began hunting large game more often and dug camas and other roots in distant, well-watered regions such as Smith Prairie, Camas Prairie on Wood River, and other places in southeastern Idaho. Large game hunted here were deer, antelope, mountain sheep, and several types of bear.

By A.D. 1700 the horse had diffused north from Spanish territory and reached the Shoshone-Bannock somewhat before it reached central and northern Idaho. Although not all people who adopted the horse were equally affected, in most cases the effect was revolutionary. As in northern and central Idaho, the horse was quickly integrated into the Shoshone-Bannock way of life and drastically modified their economic and political institutions. Groups of greater political scope emerged, and class differences began to appear as certain families amassed great wealth in horses. Some authorities believe that the horse enabled the Shoshone-Bannock to hunt the southeastern Idaho bison to the point of extinction. As a result, they were drawn farther and farther east into the Great Plains for bison as their horse herds and proficiency increased. It has been estimated that when Euro-Americans first arrived, there were from 1 to 2 horses per individual. Considering the aridity of the Shoshone-Bannock environmnt, this is a relatively large number.

The Shoshone-Bannock horse complex resembled the northern Plains type found throughout much of aboriginal Idaho. Men, women and children were mounted on several types of saddles made from rawhide and tanned hide on a wooden or antler base. The parfleche, travois, and pack saddle were used for transporting goods by horseback. Horse trappings were primarily of rawhide and horsehair and often decorated. Selective horse-breeding was practiced, and boys were the principal herders.

The annual subsistence cycle began in the spring with some groups going into the mountains for large game and roots and others going to favorite fishing locations on the Snake River. This phase continued until mid-summer when some joined into large groups to hunt bison in Wyoming and Montana. The midsummer period was also a time of large intertribal gatherings in areas such as Weiser and the Lemhi Valley. Here fishing, hunting, and root digging temporarily supported the large numbers who came from all directions to trade. Women gathered berries, roots, nuts, seeds, and insects intensively during the spring, summer, and early fall. Birds were taken during all seasons, but particularly in the summer. The late fall was a time of intensive preparation for winter; meats and various plant foods were cached in protected, well-drained locations where people would return to pass the winter months. When necessary, some winter hunting was conducted, but in general the period from December through February was one of limited hunting and gathering.

Shoshone-Bannock fishing implements included spears, harpoons, traps, dip nets, seines, and weirs. We are told that the Shoshone-Bannock originally borrowed most of these from groups to the north, such as the Nez Perces (Figures 37, 38, and 39). Twined conical baskets normally used for gathering seeds also were used for dipping fish from small streams. Fish weirs and traps were limited primarily to locations on the Snake River, and the community usually cooperated in their construction and use. Because of the dispersed distribution of the deer population, communal hunts were rare. However, there was some communal net hunting for antelope, rabbits, and certain waterfowl (Figures 50 and 51). Waterfowl were killed with clubs or by wringing the neck. Snares and spring-pole traps also were used for birds and small game. Deadfalls, pitfalls, decoys, and blinds are reported to have been used generally by the Shoshone-Bannock (Figure 52). Rodents were smoked out as well as extracted from their burrows by the "rodent skewer," a long thin pole that was twisted into the animal's skin. Both wooden and horn bows were backed with sinew and knives and arrow tips were made of obsidian. Bowls, pots, cups, and pipe bowls were made of steatite, but bone was used for salmon spears, awls, and other small tools. Eating utensils were primarily from bison and mountain sheep horn.

Like most cultures of the aboriginal Great Basin culture area, the Shoshone-Bannock gathered and transported many types of seeds in conical carrying baskets. Twined basketry seed beaters or sharp wooden and bone seed knives were used to knock the ripened seeds into the basket (Figure 53). Foods were transported in woven sagebrush, and bark baskets were supported by pack straps of skin or vegetable fibers. The pitch-lined, water storage basket was used widely. Although most basketry was twilled, occasional coiled examples are reported (Figure 54). Food was stone boiled in baskets covered with rawhide. A mixture of sunflower seeds, lamb's quarter, and serviceberries was ground into a loaf resembling bread. Seeds were pounded and roasted in willow trays and chokecherries were mashed and sun-dried. Camas and similar tuberous roots were baked in earth ovens and formed into sun-dried root loafs. Meat was either broiled on an open fire or sun-dried.

Before adoption of the conical skin lodge from the Great Plains, the Shoshone-Bannock lived in conical pole lodges thatched with bundled grass, bark, or tule mats (Figure 55). Sunbreaks and windbreaks were occasionally used for shelters (Figure 56), and some early explorers reported seeing a few Shoshone living in caves, a practice observed elsewhere in the Great Basin. Sweat houses and menstrual huts were common and resembled those found in northern and central Idaho. Very simple, temporary structures sometimes were made by placing blankets or robes over bent willows inserted into the ground.

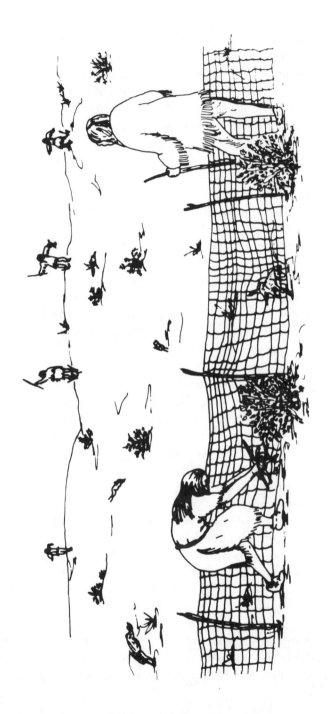

Fig. 50. Rabbit barrier net, communal hunt.

Fig. 51.   Rabbit funnel net, communal hunt.

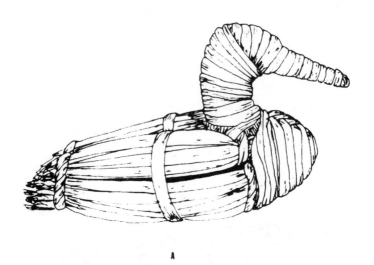

A

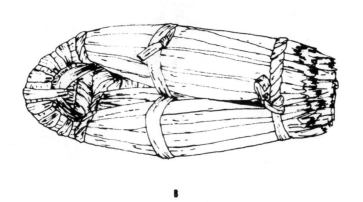

B

Fig. 52.   Duck decoys.

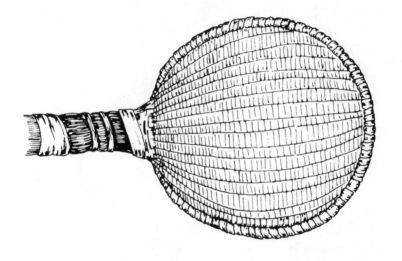

Fig. 53.   Seed beater.

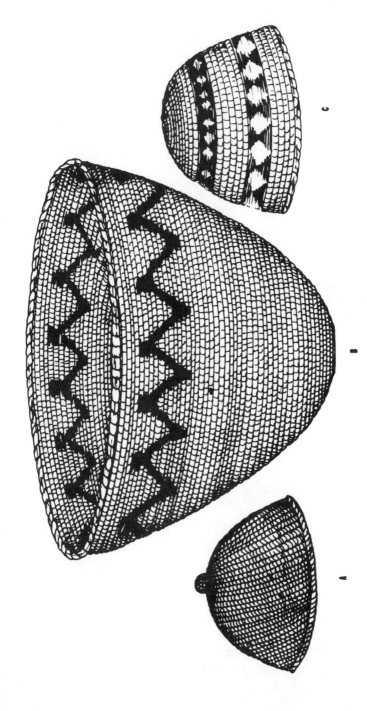

Fig. 54. Basketry: A — woman's basketry hat; B — conical carrying basket used with forehead tumpline; C — woman's basketry hat.

Fig. 55.   Thatched, conical dwelling.

Fig. 56.   Wind and sun shelter.

Although few clothes were worn in prehorse times, by the time Euro-Americans arrived, the mounted Shoshone-Bannock groups were wearing typical northern Plains buckskin dress. Men wore a long, fringed shirt of deer, antelope, or big horn sheep skin. Women wore long dresses made from the same types of hide and decorated with porcupine quills, and a girdle of dressed leather. Men wore fur caps and fringed leggings which were sometimes ornamented with scalps; women also wore shorter leggings and basketry caps. Both sexes wore robes of bison, antelope, deer, or big horn sheep skin. Generally, the skins had the hair on them, but summer robes were often dehaired. Other skins used for robes were wolf, ground hog, rabbit, and beaver. Winter moccasins had fur linings and were sometimes stuffed with sagebrush bark. In warfare, men sometimes protected themselves with armor made of laminated antelope skin cemented together with glue and sand.

NORTHERN PAIUTE

The Northern Paiute of southwestern Idaho are part of a large language (Figures 4 and 5) and cultural grouping extending south from southern Oregon and Idaho to south-central Nevada and eastern California. According to one authority, 21 distinct bands made up this widely spread group. The *Ko a'agai* and *Tagö* bands lived in Idaho, their territory centering on the upper Snake and Owyhee rivers, respectively. Unlike some bands to the west in Oregon and particularly to the south in Nevada, these two bands had annual salmon runs and relatively abundant root crops. As might be guessed, they often exploited the same resource areas as the Shoshone-Bannock, primarily fishing locations and associated root fields. They also had the same population density as the prehorse Shoshone-Bannock, but local groups rarely exceeded 50 individuals (Figure 12). Outside the favored river valleys, Paiute territory was less productive than Shoshone-Bannock territory. Indeed, it was typically desert with little water, alkaline soils, and very sparse flora and fauna. Rainfall rarely reached 15 inches annually and many areas had no rain for years (Figures 8, 9, and 10). Unlike Shoshone-Bannock territory, Northern Paiute territory had few mountains to relieve the heat and desiccation of the desert.

The Northern Paiute necessarily exploited their environment more intensively than any other group in Idaho. Large game animals such as deer, elk, antelope, and mountain sheep were quite sparse in their territory. Small game animals were, therefore, of primary importance and included cottontail, jack rabbit, mink, gopher, kangaroo rat, mouse, muskrat, wood rat, woodchuck, squirrel, chipmunk, raccoon, bobcat, badger, and beaver. Occasional trout, suckers, and several types of minnows were taken in addition to the relatively small annual salmon catch. Fowl such as doves, blackbirds, horned owls, woodpeckers, robins, bluebirds, quail, loon, duck, geese, mudhen, ruffed grouse, prairie chicken, and sage hens complemented the food supply. Insect foods included caterpillars, ants, ant and bee eggs, crickets, and grasshoppers. Seed foods included such staples as wada and sunflower, and tuberous roots such as camas and the so-called Indian potato were important also. Currants, chokecherries, huckleberries, and several other berries added variety to the spartan diet.

Although occasional references to mounted Northern Paiute are found in the reports of explorers, traders, and other early travelers in southwestern Idaho, these almost certainly referred to Shoshone-Bannock. The rare horse that penetrated aboriginal Northern Paiute territory was usually killed for food. Their arid environment and way of life simply were not compatible with the horse culture which became so important among their more favorably located Shoshone-Bannock neighbors to the east. Of course, as the Northern Paiute were removed to reservations in better-watered regions, they sometimes acquired a few horses, but this was a recent non-aboriginal pattern.

In aboriginal times, the Northern Paiute spent most of their lives in pursuit of food. In early May the people left their winter villages and searched for the first edible roots. While the women gathered roots, the men repaired the salmon traps. After the salmon run ended, the assembled fishing group dispersed into family units wandering across the land taking deer, sage hens, and other birds, and collecting seeds and roots. In mid-July the women gathered crickets, and in August and September currants and huckleberries, while the men hunted deer and elk in the mountains. Communal rabbit and antelope drives took place in September at about the same time the wada was gathered. By November people were gathering foods from temporary cache pits and returning to their winter quarters. Stored foods usually were exhausted by early spring and were supplemented by communal antelope drives and by snaring rabbits.

Most deer were hunted with dogs, who were used to drive them into an ambush beside trails and springs. Fire, scarecrows, decoys, and deer costumes were also used. Antelope were driven into corrals of sagebrush bark rope, hunting specialists sometimes magically enticing them into the corrals. Mountain sheep also were driven into ambushes or stalked by an individual. Nets, clubs, and bows and arrows were used in the communal rabbit drives, also directed by a hunting specialist. Spring-pole traps were used for birds, sage hens, rodents, and other small game, and bird nets were used to great effect, as were deadfalls and pitfalls. Ducks, geese, and mudhens were taken in communal hunts directed by specialists. Some birds were caught with bare hands from cleverly designed blinds. Smoking and rodent skewers were used to take rabbits, rodents, and other small game. Hook and line, dip nets, weirs, traps, baskets, harpoons, and hands were the basic techniques for taking fish, but there is evidence that fish poison was also used.

Sinew-backed bows of simple construction were made of juniper and serviceberry wood. Arrow tips and knives with juniper handles were made of obsidian, bone, horn, and wooden arrow tips also were used. Sometimes these tips were poisoned. Digging sticks were of mahogany or serviceberry wood. Conical baskets and basketry seed beaters were used widely with seed knives of stone. Stone pestles and mortars, as well as thin, oval metates, were used to grind seeds, roots, and meat. Spoons and ladles were made of mountain sheep horn, wood, and jack rabbit and wildcat scapulae. Coiled and twined willow cups were used in conjunction with animal stomach and basketry water canteens. Horn, bone, and stone scrapers were used for a variety of purposes as were bone awls, and broken cobbles made convenient choppers and hammers. Pack straps of skin and vegetable fiber enabled people to suspend heavy baskets from the forehead, shoulder, or chest. Deerskin and sagebrush bags and conical baskets were used for many purposes. Fire was made with the familiar fire drill found widely in aboriginal Idaho (Figure 57).

Fish, game, and insects were dried for storage, the last being roasted and pounded before storage. Chokecherries were made into cakes and sun-dried, while small mammals were roasted and eaten whole. As in northern Idaho, meat was pulverized and mixed with fat, and blood was sometimes cooked in gut pouches. Spawn eggs were mixed with seed, and marrow was obtained by splitting the long bones. Customarily, many foods were stone-boiled in baskets and meat was often broiled on forked sticks around open fires. Seeds were parched with hot coals held in baskets.

The principal aboriginal house of the Northern Paiute was a pine, poplar, or willow pole, conical frame structure covered with tule mats. Sometimes domed, earth-covered hemispherical structures as well as simple tripodal, framed structures were used (Figures 58 and 59). As among the Shoshone-Bannock, caves were used occasionally for short periods. In winter the frame, mat-covered structure was reinforced by extra matting and brush. Other structures used were sun shades (of simple lean-to construction), sweat houses (like those seen in northern and central Idaho), and menstrual or birth huts.

Before the recent adoption of skin clothing from the Great Plains, the Northern Paiute wore very little. Men wore a breech cloth and moccasins made of sagebrush bark, and women wore single or double aprons of sagebrush bark with sagebrush moccasins (Figure 60). Both sexes wore woven rabbit skin robes containing up to 50 skins, and in winter they usually exchanged their sagebrush for rabbitskin moccasins. We are told that they later adopted Plains dress from their Shoshone-Bannock neighbors. Men adopted the typical long buckskin shirt and breech cloth and two types of leggings, one that extended up to the thigh and one that came only to the knee. Women adopted long, fringed buckskin dresses, usually made from antelope hides, with belts of braided sagebrush or buckskin which they tied in front. In warfare, men made some use of armor from elderberry slats or elk hide and protective masks of buckskin.

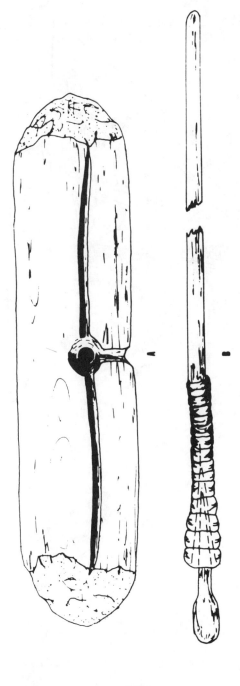

Fig. 57. Fire implements: A — wooden hearth for fire drill; B — fire drill used with bow string.

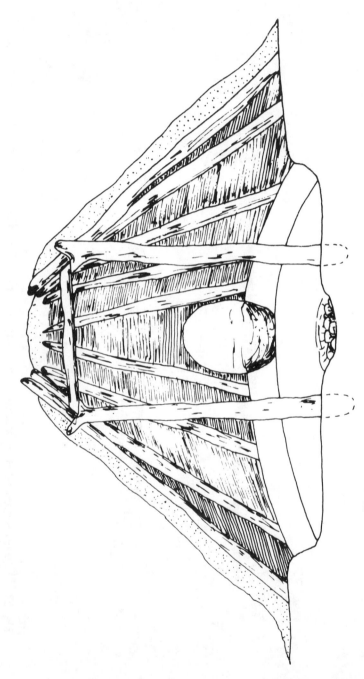

Fig. 58. Domed, earth-covered dwelling, inside view.

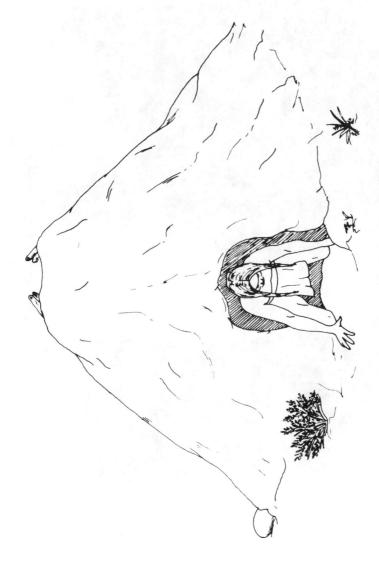

Fig. 59. Domed, earth-covered dwelling, outside view.

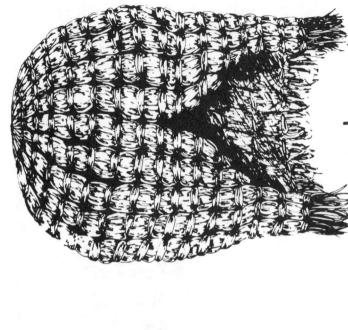

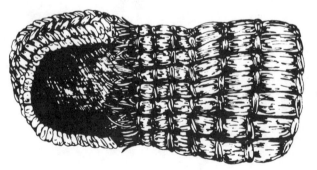

Fig. 60. Sagebrush moccasin and hat.

CHAPTER 4

SOCIAL ORGANIZATION

By *social organization* is meant the ways in which groups and individuals are organized and related to one another in society. Social organization deals with the complex interdependence among the members of a society, and produces the social order needed to survive and achieve common goals. The social statuses and roles of members may not be explicitly spelled out in any given society, but they are implicit in interpersonal relations. This chapter will attempt to clarify the statuses, roles, institutions, and other elements comprising the social organization of Idaho's aboriginal societies. In the following pages the available information will be summarized for each of the six groups described above — the Kutenai, Kalispel, Coeur d'Alene, Nez Perces, Shoshone-Bannock, and Northern Paiute.

KUTENAI
Influence from the Great Plains was particularly evident among the Kutenai in their political organization. One authority believes that the Kutenai bands (a *band* is a territorially-based group of related families led by a headman) were unified under a single authority. Other sources suggest only a tendency in this direction in that the so-called Tobacco Plains Band was dominant during warfare among the Upper Kutenai. In reality, there were at least eight different bands among the Kutenai. The Upper Kutenai bands manifested much greater Plains influence than the Lower and were permanently allied into a *composite band*, i.e., a politically unified group of bands led by a council and temporary head chief. The Lower Kutenai were organized into autonomous band units.

Although they probably allied with certain Interior Salishan groups such as the Flathead when fighting the Blackfoot in the Plains, the Kutenai had few close political allies. Some sources suggest that they occasionally cooperated with the neighboring

107

Kalispel and Coeur d'Alene to the south and west.

Contrary to popular opinion, the political leaders of Idaho's aboriginal cultures did not resemble the more powerful *chiefs* of politically-unified tribes found in the Great Plains. In its most usual sense, *chief* indicates a political leader of considerable stature, whereas *headman* indicates a local leader with little authority. Headmen were more common than chiefs in aboriginal Idaho.

Leaders of the aboriginal Kutenai were of several types. There was a general band leader, sometimes called the *head chief,* among the Upper Kutenai, and he resembled the powerful Plains chief more than any other Kutenai leader. Other leaders included the *war leader,* an assistant to the head chief who was sometimes called the *guide chief,* and the *hunt leader.* The war leader exercised his office primarily during time of war, because he was thought to have important "power" or ability in warfare. The major requirement, of course, was success, and as long as he had a winning record, all was well. The war leader also administered discipline in the community and represented the group in dealings with other groups. Prowess in warfare was accorded great prestige and any outstanding warrior received public admiration.

Among the Upper Kutenai, the assistant to the head chief was the most important leader for community organization. He saw that the directives of the head chief were carried out. On the march he was in charge of transportation and also supervised the scouts. He had to know the terrain well, for he chose camp sites and directed most economic activity. He also planned each day's activities, and his decisions were announced to the community by a chosen herald sometimes called the *crier.* In hostile territory the assistant head chief also posted the guards, who reported to him regularly. The hunting leader assisted him and functioned primarily in connection with the communal hunts organized largely to hunt bison.

Selection of the several political leaders of the Upper Kutenai was the responsibility of a *council of leaders.* This council was the major political body and consisted of the leaders described above plus *courtesy chiefs;* men who received honorary titles of chief or headman because of their bravery in battle.

Candidates for leadership positions had to be good providers, good warriors, well mannered, well spoken, and come from highly esteemed families. Leadership positions were frequently inherited, but this was not a rule, and a candidate always had to prove himself worthy of the office. As additional preparation for leadership, some candidates would seek guidance from a tutelary spirit. Each candidate was given an opportunity to lead, and if the people prospered under him, he increased his support among the council of leaders. When sufficient time had elapsed, the council made its decision and appointed the best candidate.

The Lower Kutenai did not accord their leaders as much power as did the Upper Kutenai, and looked with disdain on the custom of appointing courtesy chiefs. In general, the Lower Kutenai bands were more independent, and in contrast with the Upper Kutenai, no band was regarded as dominant over others. The practice is reflected in their leadership. Five leaders were distinguished, of which two were political — the *band leader* and the *war leader*, and three were economic — the *fishing leader*, the *deer hunting leader*, and the *duck hunting leader*. The band leader exercised the most power, with the war leader occupying a secondary role. This contrasts with the more Plains-oriented Upper Kutenai who accorded the war leader great prestige and power. Nevertheless, the war leader had to be a distinguished warrior even among the Lower Kutenai. The band leader was a general leader who exercised moral, political, religious, and economic influence over the community. Perhaps his strongest influence was religious, since he was also the Sun Dance leader. The three hunting leaders exercised influence primarily during communal hunts.

An important function of all Kutenai leaders was to provide a good example and exhort the people to proper behavior. Proper behavior was also encouraged by ridicule. The persistent troublemaker was sometimes exiled and not readmitted to the group until he had shown evidence of a basic change of character. Among the Upper Kutenai he would be readmitted if he performed exceptionally well in combat against the traditional Blackfeet enemy. Although there was no formal police force among the Kutenai, if necessary the community could and did exert force on the criminal. For example, relatives acted in unison to avenge murders which sometimes led to feuding between kin groups. In some cases the murderer would be challenged by a renowned warrior chosen by the community and relatives of the dead man. The challenge could not be refused, and usually the outcome was regarded as the final settlement.

Ceremonial societies were a very important part of Kutenai culture, as they were with most American Indian cultures. The Crazy Dog Society of the Upper Kutenai was one of the most important. This society helped select leaders and assisted them in the performance of their duties, and was modeled closely on the society of the same name commonly found in the Great Plains. Because of their vow never to retreat in battle, members of this society were used as "shock troops" and enjoyed great prestige. In special ceremonies when the drum (Figure 61) was beating, they would exhibit the unusual behavior for which they were known. Membership in this association called for a special ability, acquired through a vision, to talk to dogs. In battle, the leader of the society carried a ten-foot lance tipped with eagle feathers. Each member possessed a rawhide rattle and painted his body with many different colors.

A similar society was the Crazy Owl Society for women, whose principal purpose we are told was to ward off epidemics. Special power acquired in visions was necessary for membership. Kutenai religious specialists called *shamans* were also organized into a politically influential society. They were a major force in community life taking active roles in suppressing illness, crime, and similar social problems as well as in selecting leaders and directing community affairs.

A discussion of the Kutenai life cycle logically begins with a description of pre-natal observances. Many taboos surrounded the expectant Kutenai mother, because it was believed that virtually anything done by the mother was transmitted to the child. For example, a pregnant mother believed that she could not handle beads, cords, or anything that might bind lest the child be strangled by the umbilical cord during birth. Expectant mothers also believed they should be active and exercise frequently to assure an easy birth and a healthy baby.

Kutenai babies were delivered primarily by midwives,

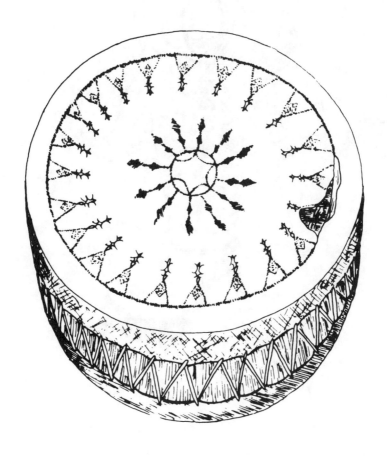

Fig. 61.   Ceremonial floor drum.

Fig. 62.   Mother, baby, and cradleboard.

although a male shaman might be called if severe problems developed. Midwives were highly regarded for their knowledge of obstetrics and took particular care when it was the expectant mother's first delivery. Three women attended her in a special birth house built for the occasion. After the baby was born, it was washed carefully, and the midwife attempted to gently shape its head and face into a desirable form. The umbilical cord was retained in a small buckskin container, and usually attached to the baby's cradleboard (Figure 62). It was believed that bad luck might result from destruction of so intimate a part of the baby.

Infants were kept in cradleboards almost constantly until they were ready to walk, and were nursed by their mothers or some close female relative until about age two, when they were weaned. If a child lost its mother before the age of weaning, it was nursed by a close female relative of the father or mother. Kutenai parents desired many children and barren couples were pitied. Childless couples could adopt children, but there seems to have been no formal adoption ceremony. Children were named for important relatives, because it was believed that they would grow up to be like their namesakes. Names were thought to be an integral part of the personality. If a person were generally unlucky, he would often take a new name. Name changing was a simple matter, done merely by announcing that henceforth the person would be known by a new name.

Children were often under the close care of older children or grandparents. Authority among them was by order of birth, a fact reflected in the different kin terms used when addressing older and younger siblings. Kutenai children were rarely punished as infants, but if strong discipline was required, it was usually administered by parents. In keeping with the bilateral kinship system of the aboriginal Kutenai, the child's relatives on both sides of his parentage cooperated in his education. By age two, the child was doing small chores, and by age six male children were participating in hunting and fishing with their grandfathers, fathers, uncles, and other male relatives. By the time he was ten years old, a boy was expected to be able to kill bison calves and fawns, and most had learned to make their own bows by this time. The more serious lessons of life were imparted to boys by their fathers and fathers' brothers. Special emphasis was given to silence and reticence in formal social situations, since boisterous behavior and loud talking or laughing were discouraged around adults.

By the time they were six years old, girls were participating in many adult female tasks such as digging roots and fetching water. Grandmothers, mothers, and aunts strongly encouraged a positive attitude toward work and saw that girls became familiar with the facts of childbirth and reproduction very early in life. Moral instruction may well have been stronger for the girl than for the boy, special emphasis being given to self-reliance and self-control. As soon as girls reached puberty, they were isolated from the rest of society and given special care and instruction for a full week. It was believed that her behavior during this critical transition period would determine the kind of person she would be as an adult. The more socially prominent families usually were more careful to observe these precautions than were less important families.

Young Kutenais, particularly boys, were sent out at puberty to seek a tutelary spirit. They sought a vision that would let them know what their specialty, or "power," would be in life. There was a belief among the Kutenai that most individuals had special abilities to be good hunters, fishermen, chiefs, or shamans, and that a portion of such ability came from a vision. Therefore, the vision quest was a critical part of a youth's education and can be equated with a high school or college degree in Euro-American society.

Marriage could occur at any time after puberty, but was usually postponed until about age 17. Although elopement occurred, most marriages were arranged as contracts between two families. The marriage ceremony consisted of the exchange of presents between the relatives of the bride and groom, and the marriage was legalized by public recognition of the couple's cohabitation.

Marriage ushered in broad, continuous cooperation between the relatives of the bride and groom. The couple normally moved in with the parents of the bride, a practice known as *matrilocal residence.* Later they might move to the home of the groom *(patrilocal residence)* for lengthy periods, but we are told that their primary residence was with the bride's relatives. The groom was always anxious to assist his parents-in-law and to show them his ability as husband, provider, and warrior. Often he would give them gifts obtained from hunting or possibly from war parties into the Great Plains. However, the groom and mother-in-law always avoided speaking to one another or being in the same room together, and the wife acted as intermediary between them. This custom, which is common among North American Indians, is called *mother-in-law avoidance*, and functions to forestall conflict between a man and his mother-in-law, who often live closely together.

As the years passed, a man's family would increase as his elderly and unmarried relatives joined him. Normally his own parents would join him when they grew old, and they played an important part in family affairs, particularly in subsistence activities and child care. These extended family households often were economically self-sufficient and large enough to comprise whole settlements.

Households occasionally would break up because of the death of one of the spouses, or through divorce, which was fairly common and could be initiated by either spouse. The primary reasons given for divorce were adultery or incompatibility. Remarriage was usually quick and rarely produced any disturbance in the lives of the children. Not only were familiar relatives present to help the children adjust, but the husband's other wives (most rich men had several wives) or his brother's wives would assume responsibility for them. The fact that Kutenai children called their father's brothers "father," their mother's sisters "mother," and their father's other wives "mother," facilitated this arrangement. The Kutenai child also addressed his cousins as if they were his brothers and sisters. Unlike most Euro-American children who tend to live in isolation from most of their relatives, the Kutenai child was surrounded by a large group of close relatives.

The great depth and flexibility of the Kutenai family and kinship system can be seen in other ways. After a formal period of mourning for his wife, a man usually married his wife's sister. Conversely, a widow often married her husband's brother. These practices are called the *sororate* and *levirate*, respectively. By remarrying in this way, the many established patterns of cooperation between relatives of the bride and groom were preserved. Adjustments to a parent's death also was much easier for the child under such arrangements. Normally, remarriage in this manner was on a basis of seniority, i.e., the surviving spouse was required to marry the oldest unmarried brother or sister of the dead spouse. The levirate appears to have been an integral part of aboriginal Kutenai life since it is imbedded in their kinship system, in that the terms for brother-in-law and sister-in-law describe them as potential husband and wife. When one considers the early average death age for American Indian men, many wives must have been prematurely deprived of their husbands. The levirate was a type of insurance system which insured that a man's wife or wives and offspring would be cared for if he died prematurely. The security and predictability this custom guaranteed was of great value to a people living at the hunter-gatherer level of subsistence.

Although age brought prestige and power to the Kutenai individual in the form of chiefship and other important offices, few lived to great age. The shaman gave those who were terminally ill the formal prognosis of death, at which time the sick person would give his medicine bundle to a friend as a sign that he knew. He was not removed from his home until after death, but this time, the lodge poles, flooring, and tent pegs were destroyed in the case of a male, and the carpetry, flooring and tent cover in the case of a female. If a chief died, the band moved to a new location. Close relatives of the deceased showed their mourning by their unkempt appearance. A man would bob the tail and mane of his horse and wear unsightly clothes, and a woman would not comb her hair and also wore unsightly clothes. The corpse was wrapped in a robe and buried quickly by a small party of volunteers on the day of death if possible. Some say that the corpse was buried on its back with the arms at the sides in an unmarked grave, but others say that the corpse was flexed and buried on its side. Cairns of stone sometimes marked the grave.

KALISPEL

The Kalispel politically resembled other Plateau cultures more closely than the Kutenai. They, like their Coeur d'Alene allies to the south and other Salishan-speaking peoples to the west, were divided into a number of closely interrelated, autonomous villages. Thus, they were not a tribe in the political sense. In each village there was a council of outstanding people, including both men and women, who chose two formal leaders or *headmen*. The principal headman had a herald and carried a staff as an insignia of his office. The assistant headman was chosen by the principal headman and often was his relative. Sometimes this headman has been called a subchief and his superior a headchief, but such terms exaggerate their power.

Generally, village headmen among the Kalispel possessed little authority. They led by persuasion more than by force and received payment in the form of prestige rather than economic returns. Although they were usually men of means, they were not always the richest in the village. Among their principal duties were arbitration of disputes, giving advice, and setting an example for the community by their good behavior. In most cases the principal headman decided serious matters in conjunction with the village council. The assistant village headman normally carried out orders given by the principal headman and saw that the village ran smoothly. He was responsible for seeing that the horses were adequately herded and that sufficient wood was gathered for the village at all times. During bison hunts on the Plains, his authority was much greater.

The position of headman was not hereditary, but was filled by election by the village council. In some cases the principal headman would be succeeded by the assistant headman, and sometimes a son succeeded his father, but this rarely continued for more than three generations without a change. The qualities sought in a headman were wisdom, social influence, oratory, bravery, fidelity, dignity, wealth, and a striking physical appearance. It was believed that headmen should always maintain self control and be resourceful. No examples are available of headmen being removed from office, but the village council presumably had this power. Although a headman might have a large personal following of relatives and friends, the council could override their influence in cases of popular dissatisfaction with a headman. If the council could not control the relatives and friends of a headman, and if there was dissatisfaction from other quarters, the resulting quarrel would sometimes break up a village.

In cases of theft and murder the headman's influence was crucial. When a murder was committed, the murderer usually would flee and stay in hiding until a settlement had been reached. The wishes of the victim's relatives and the murderer's relatives had to be reconciled with the wishes of the village council, and the headman's persuasive powers were put to the test at such times. Settlements normally were in terms of wealth and the headman saw that a reasonable price was set and that all parties agreed to it before the incident was closed.

From time to time the headman had to discipline unruly members of the community. Exile was his principal weapon, but more often a strong public rebuke was sufficient. Territorial rights were well developed among the Kalispel, and the headman was the village's main guardian. He also gave permission for strangers to use village economic resources, such as root fields.

Introduction of the horse produced some political centralization and strengthened the position of headman, but there was very little change compared to the Upper Kutenai and Nez Perces. The impression is that the Kalispel remained relatively decentralized politically with few class and rank distinctions. They retained an overwhelmingly Plateau orientation despite a small amount of borrowing from the Plains. Their limited number of horses, village autonomy, and apparent absence of any warrior societies similar to the Crazy Dog Society of the Upper Kutenai, reinforce this conclusion.

Like the aboriginal Kutenai mother, the expectant Kalispel mother observed many rules to protect both her health and that of her baby. She bathed frequently, exercised vigorously, and ate small meals, particularly when pregnant for the first time. Kindness to animals was encouraged, because it was believed that their anger could hurt the developing baby in various ways; similarly, an expectant mother avoided looking at ugly babies and corpses. Certain foods, such as pheasant, were avoided because they were thought to cause convulsions in the child.

At birth the mother was secluded in a special hut and was assisted by a midwife and older female relatives. The husband was not permitted to be present at the birth. Kalispel midwives had special supernatural powers that aided them in their tasks, but they also used herbs and physical techniques in aiding delivery, and fed the mother special foods that were supposed to stimulate sufficient milk for the newborn baby. Shortly after birth the baby was bathed and had his head and face shaped gently to desired proportions.

After about four days the mother's confinement ended and she began to care for the baby. If children could not be nursed properly, wet nurses were employed, and if the mother died, the baby would be adopted by one of the mother's close female relatives. Shortly after birth a feast was held where presents were given to the baby and a name was bestowed on him. Usually names were taken from prominent family ancestors and given at a feast by the grandfather. However, names were often changed several times in the course of a lifetime. These customs were observed more for first-born than for later children.

As with the Kutenai, the umbilical cord was saved and attached to the cradleboard in a small hide container. The cradleboard was relatively short, made of cedar or cottonwood, covered with buckskin, and lined with fur. The small size of the cradleboard eliminated much of the head flattening typical of other groups who bound the child tightly to longer cradleboards. Children were kept in cradleboards until they were ready to walk.

Fraternal twins were treated with special care because of a fear that one would die young. It was also believed that the female twin would have great supernatural power.

Infants began learning the tasks of adults very early in life. Toys included digging sticks for girls and bows and arrows for boys. Girls learned to fetch water, tan hides, sew clothes, dig and bake roots, and also learned baby care through first playing with dolls and later caring for their younger siblings and cousins. Young boys began very early to hunt small game in the company of their fathers and other male relatives who constantly encouraged them in moral behavior and in learning all the techniques of hunting and trapping. Boys and girls participated in these tasks with their siblings and cousins, all of whom were referred to and treated as brothers and sisters. They were supervised by parents, aunts and uncles, grandparents, and great-uncles and aunts, who were all called by the same terms used for parents and grandparents. Neither side of the child's family was favored over the other in this respect. The father's and mother's relatives were of equal importance to the child throughout his life, in contrast to many societies with a unilateral kinship system, where either the father's or the mother's relatives took primary responsibility. Examples of the latter are found in the Great Plains, for instance among the Crow.

At the outset of puberty, the girl was isolated from the view of the community and attended carefully by her mother, an old woman, or other close female relatives. Great care was taken with her every action because she was thought to be very pliable at this time, and her treatment during this critical phase of her life would determine the kind of adult she would be. She was encouraged at all times to occupy herself with useful tasks, such as basket weaving, exercise, and prayers for health and old age. At this time, she was given special new clothes and began wearing her hair in a new style. About a week after the onset of puberty, she took a last ritual bath and returned to the community, where she was now regarded as a young woman. Although boys are said to have received special training at adolescence, they received nothing like the special attention given girls at this time. At about this same time both boys and girls were sent out to acquire visions from tutelary spirits. As among the Kutenai, these were regarded as essential for a successful life.

Although girls could marry after they had reached puberty, most did not for several years. Elopement did occur, but marriages were usually arranged. When a young man was attracted to a girl he let his parents know, and they appointed an intermediary to talk to the girl's family. The girl's family rarely undertook a marriage proposal itself. If the girl's family regarded the suitor and his family favorably, they set a date for the ceremony. A headman or chief normally officiated and relatives from both families usually were present. The newlywed couple usually moved in with the groom's parents at first and later alternated between the groom's and the bride's homes.

Normally, marriage was a contract between the families as well as the spouses. Broad cooperation between in-laws normally grew out of a marriage and both sides were reluctant to dissolve it. Observation of both the levirate and sororate were primary methods of preserving such ties. If a husband died, his oldest unmarried brother stepped into his place; likewise, if a wife died, her oldest unmarried sister became the wife of her former brother-in-law. The kin terms used for brother-in-law and sister-in-law reflected the fact that they were potential spouses. If the surviving spouse wished to marry someone other than a sibling of his dead spouse, it was necessary that permission be secured from the dead spouses's relatives. Divorces were obtained primarily for reasons of barrenness or incompatibility.

Aboriginal Kalispel families, particularly those of prominent persons in the community, often were quite large. Multiple wives were common for richer, more prestigious men. In the case of a multiple marriage, the first wife exercised substantial authority over her husband's later wives, all of whom lived in a single, large house. The customary addition of grandparents and other, more distant relatives helped swell the size of these extended families considerably. Most households of this size were self-sufficient economically and often comprised a whole settlement. The women and girls formed continuing work groups just as did the men and boys.

By Euro-American standards, death came early to most Kalispel. Shamans could usually detect when an illness was terminal and ceased their efforts to cure the ill person. It is said that a Kalispel would confess his misdeeds to someone before death, but this might have been a result of Catholic influence. Once a person had died, his corpse was removed from the house straightaway and placed on a raised platform or in a tree. Highly ceremonialized weeping by female relatives began immediately. It is not known if the corpse was bathed, but it was given new clothes, and its hair was combed ritually. We are told that the corpse was then wrapped and tightly bound in tule matting or deer hide and buried early in the morning of the day after death. Graves were located in any convenient spot and dug by friends and relatives, who threw valuables in after the corpse had been deposited. The corpse was usually buried on its back. Shamans performed a ceremony to ensure that the dead would not return, and the grave was marked with a wooden marker.

After the funeral, most of the deceased's property was destroyed except for the best clothing which was saved for his children. His sweat house was always destroyed. Mourning was obligatory and lasted for about one year. During this time restrictions were most severe for spouses, for example, women were expected to cut their hair short and wear unattractive clothes. The name of the deceased was not mentioned, and singing, dancing and other festive displays were discouraged.

COEUR D'ALENE

Politically, the Coeur d'Alene differed from the Kalispel in that they were more centralized and had stronger leaders. At the village level, however, there were many similarities. All villages had a council with both men and women members. Larger villages had principal and assistant headmen who, like Kalispel headmen, regulated community economic, social, and religious affairs. Persuasion and public opinion comprised the bulk of their power with exile, the strongest sanction, being reserved for unresolved, serious offenses such as murder. In contrast to the Kalispel, Coeur d'Alene villages were formally grouped into three bands, one on the Spokane River, a second on the Coeur d'Alene River, and a third on the St. Joe River.

Like the Upper Kutenai, composite bands were found among the aboriginal Coeur d'Alene, but overall political unification did not develop until the time of the missionaries, treaties and reservations. The composite band political system consisted of unified groups of villages with permanent alliances. Usually such allied bands were geographically adjacent; the politically more unified Upper Kutenai, Coeur d'Alene, Nez Perces, and Shoshone-Bannock represented this type.

Although the Coeur d'Alene presumably had no social classes, band chieftainships tended to remain in particular families. Succession was not automatic, however, and chiefs were always elected (and deposed, if necessary) by a council. The *band chief* regulated the use of basic resources, gave permission for other bands to use resources in his band's territory, and exhorted the people to moral behavior. He was in charge of all interband relations, kept a calendar, and was assisted by a number of subsidiary leaders for special activities. The *war leader* also was a permanent band office, and was held by an outstanding warrior. Similarly, the various *hunting leaders* were elected because they were thought to have unusual influence over the particular game desired. The authority of the hunting leaders lasted only for the duration of the hunt. All leaders, particularly the band chief, had to be generous and were usually wealthy.

Coeur d'Alene political unity was intensified by adoption of the horse. Their subsequent involvement in the Great Plains horse culture called for broad cooperation through interband councils and strong leaders, who were often called upon to organize the large war parties and bison hunting expeditions. Especially the war leaders became more powerful, and it was but a short step from war leader to the so-called head chief and subchief system widely encountered in the Great Plains. As in the Plains, the criers and formal pipe smoking added dignity to the deliberations taking place in interband councils. When on the Plains, the Coeur d'Alene moved in a military formation, camped in the typical circular fashion, and performed their many new tasks through specialized task groupings, e.g., scouts. Their closest allies in these ventures were the Spokane, Nez Perces, Pend d'Oreille, and Flathead.

The aboriginal Coeur d'Alene apparently did not have military societies like the Upper Kutenai, but instead relied on special *ad hoc* groupings appointed as needed by the council or leaders. One authority believes that a group of military societies modeled on the Plains was beginning to develop at the time Euro-Americans arrived in the area, but the extent is not clear. It is clear that many changes were taking place in the aboriginal culture of the Coeur d'Alene at the time because of their increasing involvement in the Great Plains.

The life cycle of the Coeur d'Alene resembles that of other Plateau groups. It is said that the expectant Coeur d'Alene mother exercised vigorously and observed many restrictions in order to assure an easy birth and healthy baby. She avoided standing in doorways and looking outside, and would not fail to go through a door once she had started toward it. It was believed if the mother did not go through the door, the unborn child might be affected and not emerge easily from her body. Some believed that expectant mothers should not butcher animals or break bones. Tying knots was avoided, because it was thought that such action might cause the cord to strangle the baby. Expectant mothers also avoided looking at anything ugly or deformed lest the baby be similarly affected. We are told that a number of foods were avoided so that the child would behave properly, and animals were not angered because it was believed that they might adversely affect the baby.

When delivery approached, the mother was isolated in a special house usually several days before hard labor began. The midwife was present, usually with older female relatives of the expectant mother. Shamans sometimes assisted in difficult cases, but the husband was always excluded. The midwife assisted the mother with herbs and manipulation and encouraged her not to cry out, for it was believed to cause misfortune. She also gave the mother instructions as well as herbs to stimulate milk for the baby. After about ten days of recuperation and bathing in the birth house, the mother returned to normal activities and began to take full care of the baby. During this time the baby's head and face were gently shaped, and it was periodically bathed in a birch bark container. A number of rituals also were performed to make the baby "fleet of foot," well spoken, and a generally admired person.

After the mother and baby had recuperated, a feast was held for the child and presents were given to the baby, and the parents sometimes gave gifts in return. One of these gifts usually was an elaborately decorated, fur-lined cradleboard, which was not used for the first several months. As among the Kutenai and Kalispel, the cradleboard was carried on the mother's back. Some change in the shape of the baby's head may have resulted from the practice of binding him tightly to the cradleboard as he slept. About the time the child stopped nursing, normally about age two, he was taken off the cradleboard and encouraged to walk. He had been allowed off the cradleboard before this time for increasing periods of play and exercise. After this time and while he was learning to walk, he was carried in a skin carrying bag from which his limbs protruded.

As the infant grew into childhood, he was given increasing responsibilities. As with the Kutenai and Kalispel infant, he grew up surrounded by a large number of relatives. His elder siblings and cousins, all of whom were addressed and regarded as brothers and sisters, often cared for him when his mother was busy. He was also cared for by elderly female relatives, whom he regarded as grandmothers, and his mother's sisters and father's co-wives, whom he regarded as mothers. The father and his brothers were merged in the same way as the mother and her sisters in families of this type. These practices extended equally to both sides of the child's parentage.

Both boys and girls were given special care and instruction at the onset of puberty. As among the Kutenai and Kalispel, it was believed that what happened during this critical period determined the type of adult the child would become. Girls were quickly removed from view of the community and placed in a special house for four days under the supervision of an adult female relative. They could leave this house only at specified times and were supposed to remain busy. Special clothes and decorations were worn during this period of isolation and food was prepared in special bark dishes. At the end of the four days, the community had a celebration and the girl adopted a new hair style signifying her passage into womanhood. Adolescent boys also are said to have worn a special hair style during adolescence which was supposed to guarantee them healthy, long hair as adults.

Both girls and boys, particularly the latter, were sent out to receive visions from tutelary spirits. Special training was required beforehand, consisting of vigorous exercise, fasting, and regular bathing for boys, with less rigorous training for girls. Both sweat bathing and cold bathing were practiced very early in life because these practices were thought to make children strong and resistant to hardship. One authority states that young men seeking visions were also scarified on the arms, legs, insteps, fingers, and backs of hands, and that charcoal and white or red ochre were rubbed into the wounds to enhance the effect. The resultant scars could depict important aspects of the vision quest, but most often they were thought necessary to strengthen the youth. As with people who observe this practice in other parts of the world, they undoubtedly regarded the scars as marks of manhood.

Although the aboriginal Coeur d'Alene practiced child

betrothal, girls did not marry immediately after puberty, but normally waited for several years. If they were not betrothed, extended courtships were a rule.

Serenading with a flute and visiting girls in the evening were major pastimes for most young unmarried men. Several methods of proposing were in vogue, and chaperons regularly attended young ladies away from home. In some cases young men sought supernatural assistance in love affairs by fasting, sweatbathing, and seeking a vision, and love magic was widely practiced.

One popular method of proposing marriage began with a boy approaching a girl in the center of the lodge at which time she would stand and turn her face away from him. He sat down on the straw and talked with her, finally telling her he wished to marry her. She was not supposed to answer at that time. Then he would turn over some straw and set it on fire, and she responded by putting her foot backward and stamping it out without looking or speaking to him. We are told that he then squeezed her foot or tramped on her toes. If she said, "Why do you tramp on my foot?" he knew he was accepted and left. He then told his parents, who shortly thereafter began negotiations with the girl's parents, if they approved the marriage. An intermediary was chosen from the boy's family, and if the girl's family gave their formal approval, the boy's family would set a date for the marriage ceremony. An old man supervised the wedding ceremony during which many gifts were exchanged by the relatives of the bride and groom. Even the clothing they wore was often exchanged. A feast was provided by the groom's relatives who also gave the bride a set of new clothes at this time.

Normally the newly married couple moved in with the groom's family, and the bride was careful to respect all her new in-laws, especially her husband's mother. She was not fully accepted as part of the family until the birth of her first child, which occasioned a feast where presents were again distributed between the two families. The cooperative ties that developed between such families were protected by practice of the sororate and levirate. The sororate was mandatory for all the dead wife's sisters on a seniority basis, i.e., successively the oldest remaining unmarried sister would become the wife of the original husband. In many cases the husband would be married to several sisters simultaneously, a practice called *sororal polygyny*. As with the Kutenai and Kalispel, this usually was practiced by the richer men in the community. Inter-family ties were also perpetuated by the levirate when the dead husband's brother became husband to his brother's former wife or wives. Divorce was obtained easily, primarily for reasons of barrenness or incompatibility, but we are told that it was rare.

When death occurred a herald, or crier, was sent to announce it to the community. The corpse was not taken outside immediately, as among neighboring groups, but was left in the house to be prepared for burial, which usually occurred about two days after death. Like the Kalispel, the Coeur d'Alene had a number of relatives and friends who attended the corpse day and night while it was in the house. A typically high-pitched, stylized weeping by women began as soon as the death was announced. Those weeping and attending the corpse washed their faces and smoked periodically.

Although cremation has been reported for the Coeur d'Alene, interment was most common. Preparation of the corpse began immediately after death, when the body was washed. The face was painted, the hair was combed and the corpse was then wrapped and bound tightly in a tule or skin robe with the body flexed and the hands lying clenched on the chest. Infant corpses were buried in rabbit skin robes. When everything was ready, the corpse was removed feet first through the door by a group of friends and relatives and then slung from a pole and carried in procession to the grave. Graves were dug by friends and relatives, usually at the bottom of a rocky slope or on a river bank near the village. Speeches and eulogies were given by several people and a shaman saw that these and other rituals were performed properly. He then ended the ceremony by performing another ritual designed to protect the living from the ghost of the deceased. A simple wooden marker was placed on the grave, and the deceased's sweat house was burned along with some of his other property. Some time after the funeral, a feast was held during which the rest of the deceased's property was distributed among the guests. Large amounts of food were served at this funeral feast.

Shortly after the funeral the mourners were purified of their contact with the corpse. Many restrictions were imposed on the deceased's spouse and close relatives for about a year, and the spouse's hair was cut short and worn uncombed. No ornaments were permitted, and old, unattractive clothes were required apparel. It was not considered proper for mourners to be seen singing or laughing, and they could not mention the name of the deceased.

NEZ PERCES

The Nez Perces lived primarily in small villages along the many streams that cut through their aboriginal territory, a so-called *linear* pattern of settlement. Individual villages were identified with the small lateral feeder streams which empty into tributaries such as the south or middle fork of the Columbia River. Villages emptying into one such tributary usually were politically unified into bands and identified with the tributary. Bands in turn were politically unified into composite bands, e.g., the several bands on the upper Clearwater River made up the largest Nez Perce composite band, which centered on the present town of Kamiah in the Kamiah Valley. Three other Nez Perce composite bands centered on the present town of Lapwai, the confluence of the Grande Ronde and Snake rivers, and Alpoway between Lewiston and Clarkston on the Snake River. Some anthropologists have stated that the aboriginal Nez Perces were divided into upper and lower divisions like the Kutenai, but the best evidence at present indicates that it was only a subcultural division consisting mostly of dialectical differences in the spoken language.

Aboriginal Nez Perce villages were usually made up of several related, extended families and led by a headman. Generally he was the eldest able man in the group and was often assisted by prominent younger men. Shamans were headmen in some villages, but in all cases their powers were sharply limited by the village council which elected them. In many cases the office of headman was hereditary, but councils occasionally substituted a more effective man for the ineffectual son of a former headman. The headman's duties were to demonstrate exemplary behavior, act as spokesman for the village, mediate in intravillage disputes, and attend to the general welfare of village members. He was very influential but could not overrule the wishes of the council, which included the male family heads of the village. Women did not speak in the village council, but nevertheless managed to get what they wanted by influencing male relatives.

The band leader usually was the leader of the largest village in a locality and commonly was assisted by prominent warriors. Although they held ceremonies jointly and cooperated in certain economic activities, the most significant common undertakings for bands were aggression and defense. The band council elected leaders in much the same way as did village councils, and although succession to leadership positions was semihereditary, this pattern could be overriden by the council.

Composite band councils were made up of band leaders and prominent warriors who elected the composite band leader. Much has been said of the Nez Perce *tribe* as a politically unified entity, but there was no permanent council of all the Nez Perces led by permanent leaders. The Nez Perce head chief system was a product of the treaties and the reservation system. This is not to say that there was not extensive cooperation under powerful but temporary leaders during forays into the Great Plains. These ventures required not only tribal but also intertribal coordination. Large war parties into southern Idaho required similar leadership, but the aboriginal Nez Perces preferred not to allocate permanent power to most of their leaders. They also preferred local leadership over centralized leadership in the person of a head chief.

It has been said that aboriginal Nez Perce political leaders were of two major types. One was the *peace chief*, primarily an administrator, and the other was the *war chief,* an outstanding warrior. Both were accompanied by criers who proclaimed their statements. This common Plains pattern was developing when Euro-Americans first arrived among the Nez Perces. Political leaders could rise to eminence by developing a following through generosity, by taking scalps in war (Figure 63), or a combination of these. A candidate had a better chance if he came from a long line of leaders and an upper class family. Shamans exercised considerable political influence and sometimes became leaders because of their presumed power to prophesy and outwit rivals and enemies. Most Nez Perce leaders were compelled to behave at all times in a morally exemplary

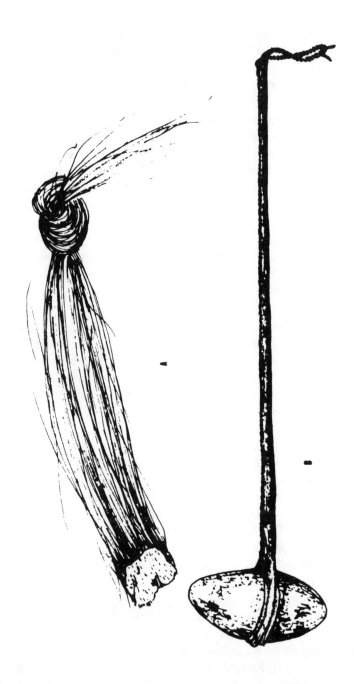

Fig. 63. War souvenirs: A — scalp lock; B — war club.

manner, to make sound decisions, and to be generous to their supporters. Their reward was prestige, rather than economic gain. Like other groups in aboriginal Idaho, serious crimes were handled primarily by groups of relatives and not by political leaders or councils, but councils could and did exile recalcitrants occasionally.

The aboriginal Nez Perces grouped themselves into several politically influential associations. For example, the powerful shamans were organized into an association for mutual support. They met periodically to perform vital rituals, conduct initiations, and solve common problems. They also had a strong voice in selecting leaders at all levels and often were quite rich. At least one such group was found in each of the larger bands. Principal warriors led an association of established and budding warriors in each of the composite bands and in some of the larger bands. They performed rituals, conducted initiations, and directed most defensive and aggressive activities. Their emphasis on bravery in warfare is reminiscent of the Crazy Dog Society of the Kutenai. They took a "no retreat" pledge and members carried a special staff in combat which they planted at a chosen spot on the battlefield and would not move from the spot until relieved or until the battle was over. They selected the war leaders and their vote in military matters was decisive. They were also influential in most political decisions. Several other associations of lesser importance also existed among the Nez Perces.

Aboriginally the Nez Perces were the most influential group in intertribal affairs in the Plateau. They roamed freely across present Oregon, Washington and Idaho with their close allies, the Cayuse, and were the main Plateau opponents of the Blackfeet who dominated the western Great Plains. Normally Nez Perce war leaders were in charge of the large intertribal bison hunting and raiding parties which often numbered more than 1,000 individuals. They were closely allied with the Flathead during the bison hunt, but the Nez Perces and the Cayuse were the major opponents of the Shoshone-Bannock raiding parties which periodically ventured north out of the Great Basin. Indicative of Nez Perce influence in the Plateau is the fact that their language was rapidly becoming the language of trade and diplomacy throughout the region when Euro-Americans arrived shortly after A.D. 1800.

Aboriginal Nez Perces spent most of their time with close relatives, and the opinions of relatives were a major influence in their lives. This began even before birth when the expectant mother's older female relatives instructed her in the proper ways of guarding her health and that of her baby. Vigorous exercise was encouraged with both hot and cold bathing, and numerous medicinal herbs were known and used freely. It was thought that touching, viewing, or ridiculing deformed animals or human beings could cause the baby to suffer the same misfortune. Similarly, the expectant mother did not tie knots or do other things symbolic of birth obstructions. Instead, she did everything that might possibly ensure a safe delivery and a healthy baby.

Nez Perce mothers usually delivered their babies in small, separate houses with the aid of a midwife or a shamaness and elderly female relatives. The young mother was also attended by her own mother when possible. A male shaman was called only if severe problems developed. Such shamans and shamanesses were thought to possess special powers in obstetrics, and their methods typically combined herbs, physical manipulation, and special rituals they obtained from their tutelary spirits. We are told that they also shaped the baby's head and feet immediately after it was delivered and took precautions to ensure that it breathed properly. The umbilical cord was retained in a small hide container and attached to the cradleboard, because the Nez Perces believed that it was bad luck to destroy such an intimate part of the baby. Relatives gave gifts and held feasts for the mother and new baby, particularly in the case of the first born child.

Babies were soon placed in cradleboards where they stayed until they were ready to walk. A mother carried the cradleboard on her back, or placed it close by so the baby could be watched easily. Nursing often continued for several years, and a mother was assisted by close female relatives when necessary. When the baby was weaned, it was given softened meats and vegetables as well as tough gristles to chew between meals. Similar to other groups in aboriginal Idaho, a ready-made adoption system existed if a mother died; the child was taken either by her relatives or another wife of her husband.

Nez Perce parents wanted many children and this feeling was shared by all relatives, particularly grandparents. Typically, grandparents cared for the children of a household after they were weaned, and very close ties developed between them. Children tended to be very formal with their parents but joked and teased a lot with their grandparents, whom they tended to regard as equals. Grandparents and grandchildren used the same kinship term to address one another, a practice that emphasized equality.

Grandchildren learned many of the basic lessons of life from their grandparents. A boy's first hunting, fishing, sweat bathing, and horse riding were usually directed by his grandfather, who was careful that he was properly instructed. Grandmothers had a similar relationship with their granddaughters. Grandparents also spent many hours recounting the numerous Nez Perce myths that were a primary means of educating the young. The child's uncles, aunts, cousins, and older siblings also took an active part in training him. The child was treated more or less equally by relatives from both sides of his parentage. Children were rarely disciplined as infants but when older, they were whipped in groups by special whippers when they misbehaved.

Nez Perces spent much of their time with siblings and cousins, all of whom they regarded as brothers or sisters. Older and younger siblings were called by different terms and respect was given accordingly, and uncles and aunts were called by the same terms used for father and mother. Typically, children were wakened very early each morning during all seasons of the year and they ran to the bathing area, where their uncles or aunts supervised their essential training. They saw that the child properly exercised and bathed in cold and hot baths, practices thought to make a child strong. Light switching of the child's body after bathing was also administered by uncles or aunts with stern lectures on proper behavior.

Nez Perce children were given names of important family ancestors because it was believed that this would favorably influence the child's development. Nicknames were common and a formal naming ceremony with gift giving was held at adolescence. Nevertheless, names might be changed at any time

Fig. 64.   Teaching a child to ride, woman's saddle.

during the life of the individual, primarily as a result of some significant accomplishment. In general, names reflected important accomplishments, tutelary spirit visions, and outstanding personal characteristics, and were regarded as private or family property.

At about age three, boys and girls began to assist in the various subsistence activities of the family. They were tied in the saddle and taken on horseback to the various hunting, fishing, root digging, and berrying areas (Figure 64), where they helped with toy bows, digging sticks, and other special implements designed for children. By age six, girls and boys were making substantial contributions to family subsistence. Special ceremonies were held at this time for the boy's first game kill and the girl's first root digging and berry picking. It was believed that if a renowned hunter or fisherman ate the boy's first game, the boy would become a good provider. Girls likewise would become good providers if their first roots and berries were eaten by an expert.

A related, important event for the child at this time was a formal, private lecture from an outstanding elder. Although he said little the child had not already heard concerning proper morals and behavior, the dignity and formality observed was very impressive. Shortly before, and for some after they reached adolescence, Nez Perce youths were sent out to seek visions from tutelary spirits. This was a major event in the maturation of both boys and girls, and if successful, it meant that they would most probably be successful adults. Conversely, they could expect only a mediocre life if they were unsuccessful in securing a vision. Many went out numerous times before receiving a vision.

The Nez Perce girl underwent an elaborate ceremony when she reached puberty. At the first sign, she was isolated from the community in a special house where she was attended by older female relatives and her mother. Friends and relatives were also notified that the girl was making this transition into adulthood. During her isolation she was urged to keep busy and think good thoughts, as it was believed that anything she did during this period would influence her life. She came outside only after dark and then for only short periods, and her meals were cooked on a separate fire. She could scratch her body only with an elaborately carved scratcher made especially for the occasion. Her isolation was ritually ended after about one week, and she was welcomed back into the community as a young woman ready for marriage. Friends and relatives gave her gifts and new clothes, and she adopted a new hair style symbolizing her change of status. Generally, upper class families took greater care with their daughters during this period than did lower class families.

Marriage among the aboriginal Nez Perces was a serious matter arranged by family heads and childhood betrothals were common. Among the most important considerations was the relative prestige of each family. Rather sharp differences of wealth and social prestige separated Nez Perce families into a three-class system. Slaves captured in war or obtained through trade were the lowest level of Nez Perce society. Normally they performed menial domestic tasks and were not given a voice in family or village affairs. Exceptions are known, however, since several male slaves rose to positions of some influence. Children of slaves were not regarded as slaves, and in general, slaves were treated somewhat like other relatives. The middle class, which contained a majority of the people, was the next level of society, and the top echelon was composed of the families of powerful leaders whose influence and prestige were augmented by wealth, primarily in horses. Membership in each class was largely hereditary. Usually, members of the upper and middle classes married within their class, but slave women were sometimes taken as secondary wives of both middle and upper class men. Slave men either married other slave women or women from very poor middle class families.

When a young man expressed an interest in a particular girl, his family met and decided if she came from a socially acceptable family. If she did, their genealogies were checked to see if they were related in any way, as marriage was forbidden between known relatives, even distant cousins. If one son had already married into the family, the marriage was especially favored, and in many instances families were linked by marriages between several sons and daughters. Sororal polygyny was common.

In other cases where a girl was desired as a wife, an older female relative of the boy began negotiations. If the girl's family reacted favorably, the female go-between moved into the home to observe the girl at closer quarters to see if she would make a good wife. During this time the boy and girl would be visiting one another and their families meeting for occasional feasts. If the girl proved acceptable and the families were compatible, the couple then began living together. If they seemed compatible and well-matched, a date was set for the ceremony and exchange of gifts. The groom's relatives gave gifts first, and about six months later the bride's family reciprocated.

During the formal gift exchanges, a number of relatives from each family faced one another across a central area and began to trade item for item. Occasionally, a rich relative would trade with two, rather than one, members of the opposite family. An element of competition existed in these exchanges, and no one was sure beforehand who would go away with the most. Relatives of the groom gave primarily male-related gifts such as horses, hunting and fishing implements, and buckskin, whereas relatives of the bride gave root bags, baskets, beads, and beaded bags. In marriages between important families, many people participated and the wealth exchanged was enormous. Careful attention was given to every detail of the ceremony. In the exchange sponsored by the groom's family the food provided was primarily meat, but in the second exchange sponsored by the bride's family, roots of many kinds were the main dish. It is important to note that although the groom sometimes gave the bride's father expensive gifts, the exchange between the two families did not favor either side. Nor were there any obvious attempts to shame the other family by giving more, which emphasized the fact that the marriage was an agreement between equals.

After the second exchange the couple was regarded as legally married. While divorces could be obtained easily, we are told that there were few, since as time passed and cooperative ties developed between the two families, both families would discourage divorce. The couples lived with those parents from whom they would gain the most, usually the groom's parents. Although there was no mother-in-law avoidance as seen among the Kutenai, the son-in-law practiced a formal respect when in her presence and was similarly careful not to laugh or joke when around his brothers-in-law. However, he joked with his wife's sisters in a rather intimate manner which related to the fact that one of them would marry him if his wife died, or if he decided to take an additional wife. Conversely, the bride showed respect for her mother-in-law and sisters-in-law, but joked freely with her brothers-in-law. This relates to the practice of the levirate, wherein the wife would usually marry the eldest of her husband's brothers should he die.

Among the aboriginal Nez Perces age brought wealth and power. The older males commanded respect widely and occupied the most important leadership positions. The death of such high ranking persons disrupted the normal functioning of social life and was followed by elaborate ceremonies. If a person thought he was about to die he normally made known whom he wished to receive his surviving property and his tutelary spirits. He also might recommend that certain sons succeed him in the various offices he held. Where this was not done, a long period of disorder often ensued as rivals competed for his property and positions. Of course, this was not as important for less powerful figures in the society.

As soon as death occurred, it was announced by a herald or crier. Close female relatives immediately began a high pitched wailing, sometimes called *keening*, and a group of relatives and friends congregated around the corpse to wail until it was buried the next day. The corpse was ritually bathed, combed, and decorated with red face paint and elaborate new clothes. The grave was normally dug by volunteers on a talus slope or high geological eminence overlooking the village, and was marked by a wooden stake. Subsequently, it was avoided. When prepared for burial, the corpse was wrapped in a robe, taken to the grave on a horse-drawn travois, and interred with a number of the deceased's favorite valuables. Occasionally, after the grave was covered the favorite horse that had drawn the travois was killed and left in the vicinity. The ceremony ended with rituals by the shaman to prevent the ghost of the deceased from returning to haunt the living.

After the burial a feast was given by the deceased's relatives who also directed the distribution of his remaining personal wealth. Horses, robes, necklaces, and implements of hunting, fishing, and warfare were among the items distributed for males; whereas beaded bags, robes, and cooking implements were given away to females. Relatives might also contribute numerous additional gifts to the assembled friends and relatives. The deceased's wishes were closely observed in the distributions which were normally regulated by prominent leaders, but everyone attending was supposed to receive something.

Relatives began mourning immediately after the death. Those who had attended the corpse ritually purified themselves, and spouses cut their hair short, wore old clothing, never laughed or appeared happy in public, and were barred from remarriage for at least one year. When a man had several wives this was not a great inconvenience, but for men with only one wife or for women, it was a period of substantial personal deprivation. Typically a surviving spouse attempted to eradicate all memories of the deceased. The deceased's name could not be mentioned and houses were sometimes abandoned or destroyed. New household furnishings were acquired and the deceased's sweat house was usually destroyed. At the end of one year, the deceased's spouse's relatives formally released the surviving spouse from mourning by providing a new set of clothes and a new spouse, if an unmarried brother, sister, or close cousin was available. If none existed, the survivor was permitted to seek a new spouse from another family.

SHOSHONE-BANNOCK

The so-called Northern Shoshone and Bannock were largely intermixed by the time Euro-Americans arrived in southern Idaho, and most of them seem to have been bilingual in the two languages. The Bannock probably came from an eastward migrating group of Northern Paiutes who were among the Northern Shoshone when horses were first acquired. Although some authorities have sought to assign the two groups separate territories, they probably occupied a common area and performed most activities together. There is some evidence, however, that the Bannock became more politically self-conscious during the signing of treaties and establishment of the Fort Hall Reservation. This may have been encouraged by government agents who mistakenly assumed that the Shoshone and Bannock of southern Idaho were distinct political groups.

To understand Shoshone-Bannock political organization, it is necessary to begin with the prehorse period which ended about A.D. 1700. Throughout this vast time period, the inhabitants of the Great Basin appear to have spent most of their time in small groups of closely related families called *patrilocal bands,* referring to the tendency of the bride to move in with her husband's family.

A very democratic style of leadership was exercised in these small bands, primarily by more experienced family heads. Although there were regional subcultural groupings, there was little political unity above the level of the patrilocal band. This form of political organization is common in many parts of the world. These bands made up regional subgroups normally identified by names based on their subsistence orientation — "mountain sheep eaters," "squirrel eaters," "sage brush eaters," etc. Regional subgroups of this type also usually occupied a small river basin drainage or other naturally unifying geographical area. Bands encountered one another occasionally in their wanderings during the warmer months and would camp together temporarily. Several families might also winter together in protected locations where food was either stored, available, or both. This occasional interaction led to repeated intermarriage between bands, and it is quite probable that regional subgroups came to speak distinctive dialects of Shoshone or Paiute.

Effects of the horse were not uniform among the Shoshone-Bannock. A few Shoshone, notably the Sheep Eater Shoshone of the mountainous areas of the Lemhi country, seem to have retained the pre-horse cultural patterns, while others dropped them rapidly. For example, the Lemhi River Shoshone quickly adopted horses and many other Great Plains cultural traits (Figures 65, 66, and 67). Like the Bannock and Shoshone around Fort Hall, they came to depend on bison and were soon known as "buffalo eaters." Two major political effects stemmed from the horse — larger local groups and stronger, more specialized leadership. The former small patrilocal bands became politically unified into larger composite bands under leaders which closely resembled the aboriginal band leaders of the Upper Kutenai and

140

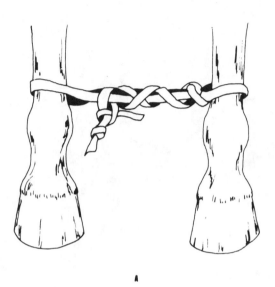

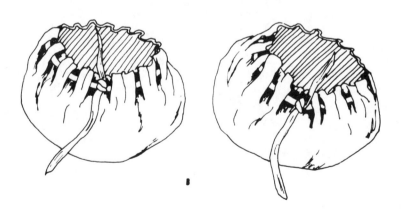

Fig. 65.   Riding implements: A — rawhide hobble; B — rawhide horseshoes.

Fig. 66.   Mounted warrior.

Fig. 67. Breaking a horse in water.

Nez Perces. In contrast to the Kutenai and Nez Perce, however, these new bands probably were not territorially identified.

Leaders among the Shoshone-Bannock horse bands were elected by councils comprised of male family heads and prominent warriors. As in northern Idaho, the position was semihereditary and carried considerable power, but Shoshone-Bannock leaders seem never to have exerted as much authority as Kutenai, Coeur d'Alene, or Nez Perce leaders. Murder and other crimes were handled by relatives, and democratic forms typical of the pre-horse period persisted in most social relations. Rarely did a band leader overrule his council, and we are told that there was much switching of band affiliation by dissident members.

During the bison hunts conducted to the east in Wyoming and Montana, however, the leaders were usually unquestioned and enforced their authority with the aid of special warrior societies closely resembling the warrior societies of the Great Plains. We are told that membership in these societies was semihereditary but validated by feats of bravery. During the hunt, members of these societies preceded the main column and others brought up the rear. They acted as scouts, warriors, and policemen making sure that the band leader's orders were obeyed.

Renowned warriors were elected to lead the composite bands, and most Shoshone-Bannock leaders came from prominent families. As in northern Idaho, such leaders were usually good orators, generous, had sound judgment, and a handsome appearance. They were elected and held office as long as they retained a large following among band members, particularly the council of family heads.

The Shoshone-Bannock horse bands of the Fort Hall area seem to have been the major political force in southern Idaho. Together with the horse bands of Shoshone in eastern Idaho and Wyoming, they were able to resist the Blackfeet and Crow on the Plains. Although often on hostile terms, they joined with other groups from northern and central Idaho for mutual protection when out in the Great Plains; one authority notes that they joined with the Nez Perces to oppose the Blackfeet. As many as 150 lodges have been counted in the large circles in which they camped during such times. Largely because of their success in the Great Plains, sharp differences of wealth and prestige soon separated the various Shoshone-Bannock groups. One authority noted the emergence of a definite upper class among them which produced a class structure similar to that of the Nez Perces. Below this group was an incipient middle class of moderately well-to-do people, and below them a small group of slaves obtained in trade and through raiding. This class structure was more prominent among the eastern groups, whereas the western groups of Shoshone, and particularly the Northern Paiute, retained the pre-horse patterns of life. The western groups lacked the prestige of the horse groups and became an occasional source of slaves and new recruits for the horse bands.

Family ties among the aboriginal Shoshone-Bannock were not significantly altered by their adoption of the horse, and life was still spent primarily with relatives. The life cycle retained many pre-horse characteristics. During pregnancy the elderly female relatives were careful to prevent the expectant mother from breaking important taboos, and care was taken that she avoid fattening foods lest the baby grow too large to deliver easily. Her diet included many roots and she usually drank heated water. She also exercised great care to protect the baby from chills, sudden shocks, and similar deleterious influences.

At the first sign of labor, the expectant mother was removed to a special house where she usually remained until after the birth of her child. Midwives, who were thought to have special powers, assisted her and usually were older women with many children. She was also attended by several female relatives who employed prayer, herbs, and physical manipulation to assist her. After delivery, the baby was washed and wrapped in fur. Sometimes the baby's father ritually bathed at this time and often would fast from the time of birth until loss of the umbilical cord which was not saved, as in northern Idaho, but buried with a prayer that the baby would grow up strong. Apparently midwives did not call in shamans during difficult deliveries, but used their special powers to solve the problem. A new mother rarely returned to the community or saw her husband for several weeks until her isolation ended with a special bath after which she donned a new set of clothes.

When the mother returned to her family a cradle was made for

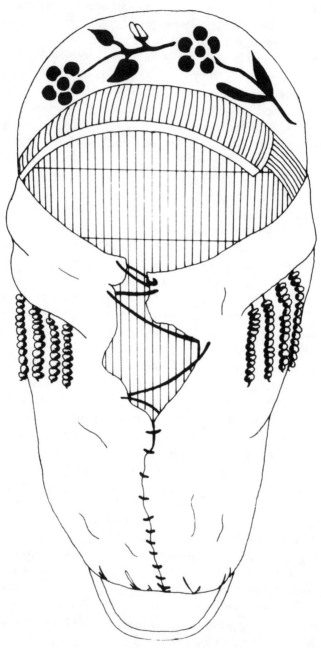

Fig. 68. Decorated cradleboard.

the baby which might be saved and used for the next baby if this one benefitted by it; otherwise the cradleboard would be destroyed for fear of harming the next baby (Figure 68). Although the baby was taken out for changing, most of his first year was spent bound to this device, and the mother either carried the cradleboard on her back or suspended it from the saddle if she were mounted. After about a year, the child was taken out of the cradleboard and carried in a robe on his mother's back. The baby was weaned at about age two when it began to talk. Men rarely took an active role in caring for infants.

When the child could walk, he was cared for by his siblings, cousins, and especially his grandparents who normally resided with the family. The aboriginal Shoshone-Bannock lived mostly in three-generation, extended family groupings where grandparents could help care for the young. Shoshone-Bannock children were indulged and rarely whipped because it was thought to break their spirit. Consistent with this was a belief that if a young boy struck his father it was a sign that he would be a brave man. In contrast to northern and central Idaho, where these practices were thought to produce strong adults, children were not required to take cold baths or submit to regular whippings. Names were given in infancy without any special ceremony, and nicknames were given later in life, as were special names for feats of bravery.

Shoshone-Bannock children, like the aboriginal inhabitants of central and northern Idaho, were surrounded by cousins and siblings whom they addressed as father and mother. All these relatives shared in the children's care and education. Important lessons were learned through playing with peers, toy bows and arrows, toy digging sticks, and dolls. It was believed that a child's dreams indicated what he would become and he was questioned carefully about them. This was especially true for children who were to become shamans. Often their dreams directed them to go to the mountains on vision quests, and parents and grandparents were careful to encourage proper attitudes toward these experiences.

Contrary to the sharp social transition experience by girls, adolescence for boys was a lengthy period of gradually intensifying changes that began early in childhood. Sometimes there was a special ceremony for the boy's first big game kill. As time went by, he spent more and more time hunting, fishing, and journeying with his peers and adult males. As he matured he would join raids into the Great Plains and, if successful, would be invited to join a warrior society in his later teens. This gradual transition into adulthood ended with marriage at about age twenty.

Girls passed through adolescence quickly, beginning with the onset at puberty and ending relatively soon thereafter with marriage. At the first indication of puberty, a girl was isolated in a small house which contained its own fire and special furnishings. For about ten days she was kept here under the care of a knowledgeable, older woman who instructed her in matters relating to marriage and family life. As in northern and central Idaho, it was believed dangerous for her to eat meat during this time, but occasional roots were permitted. Ideally only water was drunk. The girl could sleep only at night and had to gather wood every morning. Unlike the aboriginal inhabitants of northern and central Idaho, the Shoshone-Bannock did not have a taboo regarding the girl touching her body, but like them, the Shoshone-Bannock believed that the girl's behavior at this time would help determine her adult personality. Consequently, her behavior was carefully controlled. The girl donned new clothes at the end of her isolation, but no further ceremony occurred.

After puberty, courtship became an almost constant preoccupation of boys and girls. There were many formal dances where boys and girls formed trysts, and adult supervision was minimal at such times. At night boys sometimes played flutes within hearing of a girl's tent, and if she were interested she would come out to meet him. Courtship did not last long, for girls usually married shortly after puberty. Infant betrothals and other family arranged marriages were also common, and in such cases marriage to the betrothed took place more or less automatically. If there were neither betrothal nor elopement, courtship normally commenced when a boy announced his marriage choice to his family, who then selected an older relative of either sex to serve as intermediary in the negotiations. If the relative prestige and wealth of each family were acceptable to the other, the prospective groom gave the father of the bride-to-be a gift of horses which was reciprocated at the marriage ceremony. Among the Shoshone-Bannock the girl's family initiated marriage negotiations more frequently than among the groups of central and northern Idaho.

It would appear that the Shoshone-Bannock also differed sharply from most other aboriginal cultures of Idaho in their occasional practice of both polygyny and polyandry and permitting marriage among what Euro-Americans would call first cousins. Marriage between first cousins often occurs where societies are made up of relatively small, isolated groups, as for example, the Northern Algonquians, whose social organization closely paralleled that of the Shoshone-Bannock before the latter adopted the horse. Primarily, it was a way of adapting to a very limited number of marriage partners. Polyandry, the marriage of a woman to two or more men, was practiced by brothers for much the same reason, and in such cases the wife's children referred to each of her husbands as father. Both first cousin marriage and polyandry seem to have declined after acquisition of the horse because of the increased range of social contacts and size of local groups horse transportation made possible. Polygyny continued after adoption of the horse and may have increased because of the slave raiding practiced by some Shoshone-Bannock bands. It is said that older men rich in horses often used their wealth to acquire many wives. Consequently, younger men often were forced to marry very young girls or women captured during raids on other groups. Horses acquired on raids also improved a young man's wealth and chances of marrying, but desperate young men sometimes abducted married women and went to live with other bands. Where possible, however, most couples preferred to live with the relatives of the groom rather than go into exile. In such cases, the abductor usually made a substantial payment to the aggrieved husband.

Most aboriginal Shoshone-Bannock did not live to a very old age, particularly the men who were regularly subjected to the dangers of hunting and combat. Polygyny and the levirate are natural social responses to this fact. Although divorce was obtained easily, many remarriages were brought on by the early death of the husband, and marriage to the eldest surviving brother was the rule. If a man lived long enough he might find himself married to all his brother's surviving wives. Because of the preference for marriage between sets of brothers and sisters, complications produced by such practices were kept to a minimum.

Death ushered in a year-long period of mourning for the surviving spouse and close relatives, during which time remarriage was forbidden. Hair was cut short, legs were sometimes gashed, and it was forbidden to mention the name of the deceased. Mourning spouses commonly were assisted by relatives and friends in preparing the corpse for burial. It was ritually bathed, dressed in the deceased's best clothes, and tied in a robe. Cremation and open air exposure of the corpse may have been practiced occasionally by the aboriginal Shoshone-Bannock, but in most cases the corpse was buried at the closest spot. Usually the corpse was extended with the head to the west, and shamans performed rituals to protect survivors from the ghost. The funeral ended with a feast and distribution of the remaining property of the deceased. It would seem that the aboriginal Shoshone-Bannock furneral customs were less elaborate than those found in central and northern Idaho.

NORTHERN PAIUTE

The Northern Paiute of southwestern Idaho possessed a social system closely resembling that of the pre-horse Shoshone-Bannock. The extended family was the largest permanent social grouping, but the smaller nuclear family was sometimes the prevailing local group. The highly dispersed and sparse nature of food resources in the Great Basin required dispersal of people in small groups. The small nuclear and extended families were the most efficient social groupings for exploiting the limited resources of this vast region. Larger social groupings were produced temporarily during the communal rabbit and antelope drives and fish runs, where a large amount of food could be obtained at one time. At the end of these seasonal activities, however, the population again dispersed into small family units.

Like the pre-horse Shoshone-Bannock, the Northern Paiute were organized into regional subgroups named primarily for food orientation, e.g., "elk eaters," "wada eaters," etc. Such groups possessed little, if any, political significance, although they congregated occasionally for communal rituals. These regional groups were vaguely identified with a home territory, but they spent much of the year in temporary encampments. Even their winter camps varied in location from year to year. Thus, there was only a very vague division of Northern Paiute territory along political lines.

Daily life centered on the localized nuclear and extended families where the oldest able male of the extended family normally directed affairs. Euro-Americans often called this leader *Captain*, a term adopted throughout much of the Great Basin. The Captain decided when and where economic resources would be exploited, regulated intergroup relations, hosted visitors, and settled disputes. He was responsible for the general welfare of the extended family and was admired because of his exemplary behavior. Frequently, he was thought to possess special powers to cure or to locate game. Although not always hereditary, most Captains were succeeded by their sons. There were no councils of family heads, elders, or prominent members of the group as found elsewhere in aboriginal Idaho. Leadership above the family level was restricted to the seasonal communal undertakings, during which special leaders such as the *dance chief, antelope chief,* or *rabbit chief* held office temporarily. Justice was primarily in the hands of family groups who avenged murder, exiled the habitual thief, and ridiculed the habitual nonconformist.

The class differences based on relative wealth seen among the Nez Perces and Shoshone-Bannock were lacking among the Northern Paiute. Their limited wealth and small numbers made such distinctions impractical. Occasionally, slaves were encountered among the Northern Paiute by early Euro-American explorers, but it was a more common pattern for other groups to enslave them. If slaves were present, they usually were treated as another member of the family, and women slaves were taken as additional wives. Northern Paiutes captured by mounted Nez Perces, Cayuse, and Umatilla were enslaved and traded throughout much of the Northwest. Contact with the mounted Shoshone-Bannock groups to the east was extensive.

particularly during the fishing seasons when they congregated on the Snake River, but it is not certain if they were ever enslaved by them.

The limited technology of the Northern Paiute in a restrictive environment made the family the only significant social group. Practically all aspects of organized social life were regulated by kinship, which began to influence the individual even before birth. The expectant mother was instructed carefully by her relatives in all the prenatal care believed necessary by the aboriginal Northern Paiute. Little information is available on prenatal practices, but we do know that mothers tried to determine the sex of the child by magical means, that they avoided certain foods, and that they exercised regularly.

At the first sign of birth the mother was isolated in a special house containing a heated bed, and a fire was built in a pit from wood collected by the father. When it had burned down, the coals were removed and the heated earth covered with clean sand and juniper boughs. The mother was then laid on the bed. During this period the father avoided any contact with his wife and could not hunt for a month. To do either, it was thought, would endanger the baby. If he traveled in the morning, the father was supposed to go to the east and in the afternoon to the west. At the moment of birth he would take a cold bath preceded by vigorous running. He ran again after the birth and was forbidden to smoke, gamble, or sweat bathe for five days.

Normally the mother was assisted by any available older woman and by a strong man if necessary. There were no special midwives as seen among other groups. If it were a difficult delivery, a shamaness with special power would be called. After birth the baby's nose would be gently shaped, and it would be bathed before being placed in a rabbit skin robe. The umbilical cord was saved and attached to the baby's cradleboard. The first few weeks of life would be spent in a succession of basketry cradles usually woven by the grandmother. The mother was bathed regularly after birth by her attendants, drank only warm water, and used a scratching stick. During the first few days after delivery she was supposed to avoid eating meat or anything with grease and did not work at her regular tasks. A ritual bath signaled the end of her confinement, at which time she threw away her old clothes, painted her face elaborately, and like her husband, donned new clothes. These rules were observed more rigidly for the first-born child.

It is said that the aboriginal Northern Paiute feared twins, whom they regarded as a bad omen. In fact, it has been said that some twins were killed. It was also widely believed that if one twin died the other was sure to die. Deformed, illegitimate, and unwanted babies were sometimes killed. Like so many things in their life, the practice of infanticide can be understood only if we consider the limited subsistence resources of the aboriginal Northern Paiute. A child who was handicapped and could not contribute to the subsistence of the group was a tremendous burden for people living a marginal existence. Even healthy babies sometimes had to be abandoned if the group could not support them. For people who are often faced with the possibility of starvation, even one unproductive person can endanger the survival of the entire group by his use of vital resources. The decision to abandon a child, aged person, or other person is always paramount, and the individual must necessarily be of secondary importance.

Children were not weaned until they could walk, about the time they were permanently removed from the cradleboard. At about this time they were named, usually by the mother's parents. Boys were usually named for their grandfathers and girls for their grandmothers. Names were personal family property not to be taken by others arbitrarily without first seeking permission. After his naming, the child began to take an increasing part in subsistence activities. Girls learned early how to gather seeds and roots and how to carry heavy loads of wood. Boys began the life-long task of learning the habits of the many small animals, birds, reptiles, and insects eaten by the Northern Paiute. It was necessary for everyone to gather food, and the contributions of children were substantial. Usually the boy hunted with his grandfather, father, uncles, brothers, and occasionally male cousins, while girls accompanied their grandmothers, mothers, aunts, sisters, and female cousins. At times both sexes worked together on communal tasks, such as rabbit drives.

In their kinship names, the Northern Paiute tended to separate their father and mother from their uncles and aunts and their siblings from their cousins. This practice resembles the Euro-American system and is typical of cultures where families are substantially isolated from one another as they were in the Great Basin. In Northern Paiute families the ties between grandparents, parents, and children were particularly close, and ties with other relatives less close. This contrasts sharply with the Plateau groups to the north, where cousins and siblings, mothers and aunts, and fathers and uncles were regarded as equals in the kinship system. The Great Basin groups did not have closely-knit, large extended families as did the groups in northern and central Idaho, but instead had relatively smaller, independent family units. Parents and youths gathered most of the food, whereas grandparents cooked and stored it and cared for young children while parents were absent. Grandparents also instructed the entire family in traditional wisdom and morals. Children learned many basic lessons of life from the myths regularly recounted by their grandparents.

By about age 8 or 9, parents and grandparents began to question the child about his dreams, for it was believed that dreams indicated the type of adult he would be. Sometimes when he slept or when he was alone tutelary spirits imparted special messages to him. Each spirit gave a special power, e.g., a hawk was thought to give swiftness and a lizard, stealth. By about age 14 the boy began undergoing special training in which he took cold baths, made long runs, and listened to special songs his grandfather would sing to him. As his power became recognized in the family, he gradually was regarded as an adult. By age 15 the transition usually was complete and he was ready to marry.

It was thought dangerous for men or ill persons to come in contact with pubescent girls. Consequently, at the first sign of puberty, girls were isolated for about one month in a special house where they were attended by their mothers or other female relatives. In their absence, any trusted older woman was acceptable. During this time a girl was given special instruction in proper feminine behavior, and her hair was combed frequently by her attendants. She was also required to rise early in the morning, act in a dignified, demure manner, make daily runs, gather firewood for the fire in her house, and drink from a special cup. As we have seen for other groups, she could not touch her body for about five days and used a special scratching stick. She ritually bathed every five days and ended her month-long isolation with a bath, after which she donned new clothes and painted her face with red pigment.

Puberty observations for boys were less elaborate, and often associated with their first significant game kill. A boy received extended lectures from his father and other older male relatives who gave him a special bath and prayed that he would be a successful hunter during his life. Neither the boy nor his family ate any of his first kill, which was reserved for nonrelatives, particularly those who were renowned hunters. As among the Nez Perces, having a renowned hunter eat the boy's first kill was thought to improve his chances of becoming a good hunter. At puberty or earlier both boys and girls began to dream of their power, but this was not closely linked with puberty observances. As elsewhere, securing a tutelary spirit was an essential step in maturation.

Girls usually married shortly after puberty and somewhat sooner than boys. Warfare was unimportant among the aboriginal Northern Paiute and boys were not encouraged to pursue honor in battle as were Shoshone-Bannock boys to the east. Instead, they often went on extended trips visiting other groups in search of an unrelated, acceptable spouse. Their mothers exercised some control over their selection, but formal betrothal apparently was not common. If the girl was selected by his family, the boy went to her home nightly and sat quietly outside the door. He would remain until the family retired and then leave. In time and if her parents offered him food, he was accepted and moved in with them. Shortly thereafter the two families met and exchanged gifts as a means of publicly announcing the marriage. The couple often remained with the bride's family until their first child, and then moved in with the groom's family. The place of residence was highly variable among the aboriginal Northern Paiute and a couple might move many times due to economic considerations. Only through frequent mobility were people able to adjust to seasonal and annual variations in the availability of food resources.

Divorces were frequent and easily obtained among the aboriginal Northern Paiute. Although somewhat rare, they also practiced both polyandry and polygyny. As elsewhere, polyandrous unions usually consisted of two brothers married to the same woman, and their offspring regarded each brother as their father. Nevertheless, most polyandrous unions did not last long and were terminated when one of the brothers found another wife, often a younger sister of his former wife. The relative scarcity of people, the levirate, the sororate, and the preference for marriage between several brothers and sisters all contribute to the practices of polyandry and polygyny. The small, isolated family groups in which the aboriginal Northern Paiute lived occasionally produced a surplus of males in a given region. Polyandry as well as polygyny are natural resonses to such imbalances. In one sense a polyandrous marriage is a premature exercise of the levirate. Instead of marrying his brother's wife after his brother dies, the younger brother marries her before. The sororate relates to polygyny in the same way. Preference for several marriages between the children of two families encouraged polyandry and polygyny for obvious reasons. The main difference between Northern Paiute polygyny and polyandry was that polygyny was practiced for prestige more frequently and more successfully than polyandry.

Because of the rigorous life imposed on these people by their harsh environment, life expectancy was relatively low. When death occurred, close relatives went into mourning immediately, but the corpse was not removed from the house until the next day. Before removal it was ritually washed, painted with fresh pigments, and dressed in good clothes. Other adornments such as necklaces were added when available. Relatives saw that these steps were performed, but there is no evidence of the large numbers of mourners that commonly assembled during funerals in aboriginal central and northern Idaho. We are told that they did not wish to retain the corpse any longer than necessary. In some cases the corpse was cremated, but more often it was buried extended on its back in a rock shelter, on a rocky slope, or on a mountain. The ceremony ended quickly with a eulogy by an esteemed older man with a request that the deceased's ghost not return. Most of his property was burned.

Surviving close relatives cropped their hair and sometimes burned it. Women, particularly spouses, sometimes gashed their legs and spouses were forbidden to remarry for at least one year. Mourners did not mention the name of the deceased again lest his ghost be encouraged to return. It was believed that the dead were reluctant to leave their relatives and would sometimes attempt to take one with them. Young children, usually grandchildren who died shortly after a grandparent's death, were thought to have gone with the grandparent. The close emotional ties between grandparents and grandchildren make this belief understandable. Most people were careful to avoid graves, because ghosts were thought to cause illness, accident, or death for anyone whom they encountered. Considered within this framework, the remote location of graves is also understandable.

CHAPTER 5

WORLD VIEW

INTRODUCTION

In this chapter we shall depart from the tribe-by-tribe descriptions used in Chapters 3 and 4. Because of the broad similarities of world view throughout much of aboriginal Idaho, it is feasible to describe the region as a whole. The absence of comparable studies for each group also encourages this approach.

The world view, or collective value system of a culture, is the most difficult part for an outsider to understand. The functions of an arrow, dip net, or moccasin are generally self-evident, but the collective value system can be understood only through intensive study. There are several ways to explore this topic, and careful analysis of religion and mythology is one of the best. Because of their symbolic and often conservative character, myth and religion give us a view of the ways Idaho's aboriginal people thought and felt about themselves and the world around them.

At the outset, it can be said that the aboriginal peoples of Idaho viewed themselves and the world in ways similar to many other American Indians. For example, their myths reveal the well-known themes of immanent justice, bravery, generosity, and repression of emotion. They also emphasize individual autonomy and resistance to centralized authority as well as dependence on supernatural power which was thought to determine one's fate. Child rearing practices, rituals, and public exhortations by leaders constantly served to reinforce these basic values.

RELIGION IN ABORIGINAL IDAHO

Although the Sun Dance, Native American Church, Indian Shaker Church, Seven Drum Religion, and various Christian denominations are now found among Indian people of Idaho, these are recent developments. They result primarily from European influences which began filtering into Idaho at least as early as A.D. 1700, a century before the Lewis and Clark expedition.

The religions of aboriginal Idaho were based on several fundamental ideas. Foremost was a belief that there was a supernatural side to man's existence and to all of nature. It was believed that phenomena of nature such as rocks, trees, rivers, animals, birds, fish, and astral bodies could influence man's destiny in important ways. They appeared to men in visions, and a few gifted people, primarily shamans, communicated with them regularly. This belief that natural phenomena have a spiritual side is called *animism,* and the customary quest for a vision from such *tutelary* (teaching) *spirits* was common among most American Indians.

Through the vision quest, it was thought that tutelary spirits conferred on certain human beings *powers,* or what in effect were supernaturally supported abilities. Among all groups in aboriginal Idaho, it was thought that a person's power and, consequently, his tutelary spirit, were apparent in outstanding character traits or skills. Although similar, powers were more than simply abilities. They were thought to have a separate existence, and the tutelary spirit could even punish a person who broke a taboo or failed to observe proper rituals connected with his power. A person's power could weaken or act against him if he abused it, causing bad luck, illness, accident, and even death. One such abuse was not undergoing ritual cleansing before approaching a tutelary spirit. The necessary cleansing and preparation were achieved through fasting, exercise, meditation, and avoiding a number of customary activities for specified periods. Although power was occasionally obtained in unexpected visionary encounters, most boys and girls were sent on formal vision quests. Their parents and other relatives hoped that they would have a visionary encounter with a tutelary spirit who would give them a valuable power. Usually parents prepared their children for the quest by special instruction over several years, and accompanied them to an isolated location such as a mountain top. Sometimes they were given objects symbolic of the power they desired, because these were thought to encourage particular tutelary spirits to take favorable notice of the youth. Vigils could last several days and were usually repeated if unsuccessful. During the vigils the child was cautioned to keep alert, fast, exercise, and take cold baths where possible.

In a vision, the tutelary spirit normally appeared in human form, but his animal nature was also apparent to the youth. The tutelary spirit would explain the nature of the power he was conferring and could instruct the youth in a special power song, which became the property of the youth. He would use it subsequently on ritual occasions and when he needed supernatural aid. It was both a public sign of his power and a means of summoning his tutelary spirit in time of need. The youth would not discuss his visionary experience publicly, because it was believed this would weaken him. As he matured shamans would often aid him in discovering more about his power, including special ways of communicating with and securing benefits from it. He prepared a small bundle in which were kept various items symbolic of his power, and he periodically performed rituals necessary to keep his power strong. As long as he observed the proper rituals and taboos, he was assured of support from his tutelary spirit, but if he failed or abused his power, it was thought he courted disaster. At death it was thought that an individual's power sometimes wished to remain with one of his relatives and would appear to the survivor in his dream. As the youth matured, this power became more evident. For example, if he had inherited a power useful in warfare, he would be successful on the battlefield. If he had inherited a hunting power, this also would be recognized by his success. If he had inherited a shaman power, it was thought that other shamans, especially older relatives who were shamans, would know it and begin instructing him in the proper behavior and knowledge necessary to strengthen his power and acquire additional ones through vision quests.

Another basic idea in the religion of aboriginal Idaho was the concept of *soul*, a religious belief found throughout the world. Humans as well as natural objects were thought to possess souls, without which they died. The ideas of soul and tutelary spirit should not be confused by the reader. Unlike the soul, a tutelary spirit was obtained well after birth, and its loss did not necessarily bring about death. Among most aboriginal American Indian groups, it was thought that souls could be lost for various reasons, but the idea of reward and punishment of one's soul in heaven or hell probably was not present until after European religious concepts were introduced. In aboriginal Idaho the fate of one's soul did not depend very much on how he had lived. Rather, it depended more on the proper observance of rituals, and elaborate precautions were taken at death to ensure that the soul of the deceased successfully reached the afterworld. Individuals were supernaturally rewarded or punished on earth for their actions by gaining or losing supernatural power or by being harmed by a spirit they had offended, and life in the afterworld was thought to be mostly a continuation of the present life.

Shamans were the principal religious specialists in aboriginal Idaho and officiated at most rituals. Found in many cultures around the world, they gained their authority from their capacity to deal directly with supernatural figures, i.e., tutelary spirits. Whereas the average individual had one or two tutelary spirits, it was thought that shamans had many. Probably the most important function of the shaman in aboriginal Idaho was curing. We have already seen in Chapter 4 how shamans attended expectant mothers in times of difficulty and aided other persons who were ill. Other important duties of shamans included prophesying the future, locating game or other food resources in times of famine, and giving advice on individual and community problems. It should be emphasized that shamans were respected and admired for their many positive contributions to the community, and only a handful of people were able to master the difficult steps necessary to become and remain a shaman. The overwhelming majority were gifted, highly respected members of society, who left their everyday occupations in times of crisis to employ their special skills in helping people in need. Most of what they did depended more on common sense and clear understanding of human beings than on supernaturalism. Clearly, their supernatural side should not be exaggerated.

As we have seen above, most groups in aboriginal Idaho possessed rituals for birth, name-giving, marriage, sickness, and burial. Elaborate rituals also accompanied the seasonal arrival of the first salmon and roots. A winter tutelary spirit dance was supervised by shamans who directed the elaborate dramatizations of tutelary spirits in songs, dances, and impressive costuming. We have already touched on the life cycle rituals in Chapter 4, enough to know that every significant change in the life of a person involved a corresponding change in his religious or ritual status. In fact, most important events in the life of either the individual or the community were accompanied by ritual activity which was thought necessary to bring about the proper outcome. The first salmon and first roots rituals were especially so. Unless the salmon or roots were welcomed properly, it was thought that they might not return again. In various forms this fertility emphasis is found throughout the world's religions. As seen in Chapters 3 and 4, the complexity of these rituals, as well as other cultural patterns, varied considerably from the simplified forms of the Paiute in the south to the relatively complex forms seen in central and northern Idaho.

An important function of rituals in aboriginal Idaho was to validate social status which was facilitated by having community leaders, who often were also shamans, preside over rituals. Indeed, ritual authority and political authority were generally synonymous in aboriginal Idaho. Individuals who possessed skill in social and political affairs were thought to have corresponding supernatural powers. Conversely, supernatural powers from strong tutelary spirits were thought to prepare a person for positions of social and political responsibility. One of the most important themes in ritual activity was reaffirmation of the authority of such leaders and group loyalty to them. Simultaneously stressed was reaffirmation of loyalty to the group and its ideals.

Reflecting an ultimate dependence on nature for survival, most rituals included many expressions of respect for animals. In some groups, it was thought that before human beings came, animals dominated the earth and that they behaved like human beings. Although it was believed that they became mute and dumb thereafter, they still could withhold their flesh from people if they were offended. Each species was represented in the tutelary spirits who, we have seen, also gave people various powers essential to success in life. In brief, people saw themselves as living in nature, largely on a par with other forms of life. The impression is gained that people saw themselves as members of a very large community of beings which included most of nature. Needless to say, this type of world view was fundamentally compatible with their hunting and gathering way of life. As seen below, their mythology reinforced these basic ideas in many ways.

MYTHOLOGY

All societies have prose literary forms, whether oral or written. In aboriginal Idaho, as in many parts of the world, this takes the form of myths, or as they are often termed, legends. We have included our discussion on mythology with the analysis of religion because the two are closely related in many ways. Myths impart the basic values and beliefs of a society and give moral instruction to its members. They serve to explain the creation of the world and its beings, the significance of rituals and customs, and the religious meaning of birth, death, and other natural occurrences. In one sense the Christian Bible is a similar set of myths which impart basic religious truths.

In addition to their explanatory function, myths also serve as mechanisms for educating children, stimulating social interaction, and amusement. The behavior of animal characters instructs children in proper behavior and teaches them lessons of practical value, such as the habits of game animals, the location of food resources, how to use tools and implements, and the geography of their territory. Myths frequently stimulate a sense of group cohesion and pride, because they describe how a people were created and often how they are superior to others.

In aboriginal Idaho, myths were usually recounted by elders during the winter and emphasized several recurrent themes. Some myths explained the origin of the present order, i.e., how an animal, topographical feature, or customary way of doing things came to be the way it was. Others demonstrated how clever deception and trickery could either help or hinder, depending on whether they were used for group welfare or in a selfish, egotistic manner. Lessons in the grievous results of theft, gluttony, and cheating of relatives were especially common in the myths. Contests of strength and endurance reflected the high value placed on physical fitness and courage. The need for group cohesion and cooperation against outside threats was also depicted in the conquest of ogres, monsters, and cannibals. Immanent justice, the belief that the right will triumph in the end, was frequently expressed in myths about revenge, justice, and the defeat of animal characters who acted against group welfare. As in myths everywhere, magic is frequently used for well-known purposes, mostly to make a good story better and to extricate characters in the stories from otherwise impossible situations. Magical loss and replacement of body parts, magical revival from the dead, and transformation of the self occur frequently in the myths. Coyote often uses magic to transform things into their present shape. Indeed, the central character in the mythology of most American Indians is a *transformer-trickster*, who changes himself, other animals, people, and topographical features in various ways. Countless myths from aboriginal Idaho recall how Coyote, the principal trickster, changed an animal or natural object into its present form.

The trickster figure is a worldwide phenomenon, and has parallels in the picaresque novels of Spain, the fairy tales of the Brothers Grimm, Greek gods and goddesses, and the literary traditions of countless other cultures. The psychiatrist C.G. Jung (1956) provides a useful commentary on this figure:

> He is . . . God, man, and animal at once. He is both subhuman and superhuman, a bestial and divine being . . . he is in many respects stupider than the animals, and gets into one ridiculous scrape after another. Although he is not really evil he does the most atrocious things . . . . The trickster is a primitive 'cosmic' being of 'divine-animal' nature, on the one hand superior to man because of his superhuman qualities, and on the other hand inferior to him because of his unreason . . . . He is no match for the animals either, because of his extra-ordinary clumsiness and lack of instinct . . . .

In myths the trickster often acts out man's socially disruptive drives, thereby revealing the disastrous results of violating conventional mores. There is an implication in most myths that man has progressed beyond this state of amorality and unreason to become a superior being. In fact, children are explicitly encouraged to learn how to behave properly from the clumsiness and foolishness of Coyote who lived before the people came in a time sometimes called the pre-cultural era.

REFERENCES CITED

AOKI, HARUO
1962   Nez Perce and Northern Sahaptin: a binary compari-
        son. *International Journal of American Linguistics*
        28(3):172-182.

1966   Nez Perce and Proto-Sahaptin kinship terms. *Inter-
        national Journal of American Linguistics* 32(4):357-368.

1970   Nez Perce grammar. *University of California Publi-
        cations in Linguistics* 62.

BAHAR, HUSHANG
1955   Pend d'Oreille kinship. Unpublished M.A. thesis,
        University of Montana, Missoula.

BAILEY, VERNON
1936   The mammals and life zones of Oregon. *U.S. Depart-
        ment of Agriculture, Bureau of Biological Survey* No.
        55.

BAKER, PAUL E.
1955   The forgotten Kutenai. Boise: Mountain States Press.

BOAS, FRANZ
1899   Anthropometry of Shoshonean tribes. *American
        Anthropologist* 1:751-758.

1918   Kutenai tales. *Bureau of American Ethnology,
        Bulletin* 49:1-387.

1919   Kinship terms of the Kutenai Indians. *American
        Anthropologist* 21:98-101.

BRIMLOW, GEORGE FRANCIS
1938   The Bannock Indian war of 1878. Caldwell: Caxton
        Printers.

BROPHY, WILLIAM A. and SOPHIE D. ABERLE
1966   The Indian: America's unfinished business. Norman:
        University of Oklahoma Press.

BROWN, WILLIAM C.

1926   The Sheepeater campaign, Idaho — 1879. Boise: Syms-York.

1961   The Indian side of the story. Spokane: C.W. Hill.

BUTLER, B. ROBERT

1968   A guide to understanding Idaho archaeology. Pocatello: Idaho State University Museum.

CAPPANNARI, STEPHEN C.

1950   The concept of property among Shoshoneans. Unpublished Ph.D. dissertation, University of California, Berkeley.

CHAMBERLAIN, A.F.

1893   The coyote and the owl. *Memoirs of the International Congress of Anthropology, Chicago.* pp. 282-284.

1894   A Kootenay legend. *Journal of American Folklore* 7:195-196.

1893-   Notes on the Kootenay Indians. *American Antiquarian*
1895   *and Oriental Journal* 15:292-294; 16:271-274; 17:68-72.

1901a   Kutenai basketry. *American Anthropologist* 11:318-319.

1901b   Kootenay "Medicine-Man." *Journal of American Folklore* 14:95-99.

1901c   Kootenay group-drawings. *American Anthropologist* 3:248-256.

1902   Geographic terms of Kootenay origin. *American Anthropologist* 4:348-350.

1905   The Kootenay Indians. *Annual Archaeological Report, Report of the Minister of Education of Canada.*

1907   Kutenai. *Bureau of American Ethnology, Bulletin* 30(1):740-742.

1909   Note sur l'influence exercee sur les Indiens Kitonaga par les missionaries catholiques. *Revue des Etudes Ethnographiques et Sociologiques* 2:155-157.

COOK, SHERBURNE F.
1955   The epidemic of 1830-1833 in California and Oregon. *University of California Publications in American Archeology and Ethnology* 43:303-326.

CRAIG, WALLACE, *et al.*
1963   A human resources survey of the Nez Perce tribe. Unpublished Manuscript, North Idaho Indian Agency, Lapwai, Idaho.

CROCKETT, JOY
1923   The operations of the Hudson's Bay Company in old Oregon. Unpublished M.A. thesis, University of Idaho, Moscow.

DAVIS, RAY F.
1952   Flora of Idaho. Dubuque: William C. Brown.

DAVIS, WILLIAM B.
1939   The recent mammals of Idaho. Caldwell: Caxton Printers.

D'AZEVEDO, WARREN L., *et al.*, eds.
1966   The current status of anthropological research in the Great Basin: 1964. *Desert Research Institute, Technical Report Series 5-H, Social Science and Humanities Publication*, No. 1.

DE SMET, PIERRE JEAN
1905   Letters and travels of Father Pierre Jean de Smet. New York: Frances P. Harper.

DOBYNS, HENRY F.
1968   Therapeutic experience of responsible democracy. *In* The American Indian today, Stuart Levine and

Nancy Lurie, eds., pp. 171-187. Deland: Everett-Edwards.

DORN, EDWARD
1966   The Shoshoneans: the people of the Basin-Plateau. New York: William Morrow.

DOWNS, JAMES F.
1966   The significance of environmental manipulation in Great Basin cultural development. *In* The current status of anthropological research in the Great Basin, Warren L. d'Azevedo, *et al.*, eds., pp. 39-57.

DOZIER, JACK
1961   History of the Coeur d'Alene Indians to 1900. Unpublished M.A. thesis, University of Idaho, Moscow.

DRIVER, HAROLD E.
1961   Indians of North America. Chicago: University of Chicago Press.

DRURY, CLIFFORD
1936   Henry Harmon Spalding. Caldwell: Caxton Printers.

1958   Spalding and Smith on the Nez Perce mission. Glendale: Arthur H. Clark.

DUSENBERRY, VERNE
1959   Visions among the Pend d'Oreille Indians. *Ethnos* 24: 52-57.

EGGAN, FRED, ed.
1955   Social anthropology of North American tribes. 2nd edition. Chicago: University of Chicago Press.

EMERSON, RALPH L.
1962   A chronology and interpretation of nineteenth-century Plateau culture history. Unpublished M.A. thesis, University of Washington, Seattle.

EVANS, JOSHUA T.
1938   The northwest Shoshone Indians under tribal organi-

zation and government. Unpublished M.A. thesis, Utah State University, Logan.

EWERS, JOHN
1955   The horse in Blackfoot culture. *Bureau of American Ethnology, Bulletin* 159.

FOWLER, DON D.
1966   Great Basin social organization. *In* The current status of anthropological research in the Great Basin, Warren L. d'Azevedo, *et al.*, eds., pp. 57-75.

GATES, M.E.
1900   A visit to the northern reservations in Oregon and Montana. *Leaflets of the Museum of the American Indian, Heye Foundation* 17:57-61.

GIBBS, GEORGE
1860   The natural history of Washington Territory and Oregon. Collected by J.C. Cooper and George Suckley. New York: Bailliere.

GOSS, JAMES A.
1968   Culture-historical inference from Utaztekan linguistic evidence. *In* Utaztekan prehistory, Earl H. Swanson, Jr., ed., pp. 1-42. *Occasional Papers of the Idaho State University Museum*, No. 22.

GRAHAM, CLARA
1963   This was the Kootenay. Vancouver, B.C.: Evergreen Press.

HAINES, FRANCIS
1938   The northward spread of horses among the Plains Indians. *American Anthropologist* 40(3):429-437.

1955   The Nez Perces. Norman: University of Oklahoma Press.

HANDY, HENRY W.
1948   History of the Roman Catholic church in Idaho. Unpublished M.A. thesis, University of Idaho,

Moscow.

HARBINGER, LUCY JANE
1964   The importance of food plants in the maintenance of
        Nez Perce cultural identity. Unpublished M.A. thesis,
        Washington State University, Pullman.

HARRIS, JACK S.
1940   The White Knife Shoshoni of Nevada. *In* Accultura-
        tion in seven American Indian tribes, Ralph Linton,
        ed., pp. 39-118. New York: D. Appleton-Century.

HART, C.P.
1866   Paiute herbalists. *Proceedings of the American
        Association for the Advancement of Science* 35:
        330-331.

HENRY, ALEXANDER
1897   New light on the history of the greater northwest:
        the manuscript journals of Alexander and David
        Thompson. Elliott Coues, ed., New York: F.P. Harper.

HENSHAW, H.W. and C. THOMAS
1907   Bannock. *Bureau of American Ethnology, Bulletin*
        30(1):129-130.

HENSHAW, H.W. and J. MOONEY
1910   Paiute. *Bureau of American Ethnology, Bulletin*
        30(2):186-188.

HEWES, GORDON
1947   Aboriginal use of fishery resources in northwestern
        North America. Unpublished Ph.D. dissertation,
        University of California, Berkeley.

HOEBEL, E.A.
1938   Bands and distributions of eastern Shoshoni.
        American Anthropologist 40:410-413.

HULTKRANTZ, AKE
1956   Configurations of religious belief among Wind
        River Shoshoni. *Ethnos* 21:194-215.

ISCH, FLORA MAE BELLEFLEUR
1948   The development of the upper Flathead and Kootenai country. Unpublished M.A. thesis, University of Montana, Missoula.

JENNESS, DIAMOND
1932   The Indians of Canada. *National Museum of Canada, Bulletin* 65.

JONES, J.A.
1955   Kalispel law. *Proceedings of the Indiana Academy of Science* 65:50.

JOSEPHY, A.M., JR.
1965   The Nez Perce Indians and the opening of the northwest. New Haven: Yale University Press.

JOHNSON, OLGA W.
1969   Flathead and Kootenay: the rivers, the tribes, and the region's traders. Glendale: The Arthur H. Clark Co.

JUNG, C.G.
1956   On the psychology of the trickster figure. *In* The trickster: a study in American Indian mythology, by Paul Radin, pp. 195-211. New York: Bell Publishing Company.

KELLY, ISABEL T.
1938   Northern Paiute tales. *Journal of American Folklore* 51:363-438.

KENNEDY, K.A.R.
1959   The aboriginal population of the Great Basin. *Records of the University of California Archaeological Survey* 45:1-84.

KROEBER, A.L.
1939   Cultural and natural areas of native North America. *University of California Publications in American Archaeology and Ethnology* 38.

LAIDLAW, SALLY JEAN
1960   Federal Indian land policy and the Fort Hall Indians. *Occasional Papers of the Idaho State College Museum*, No. 3.

LEVINE, STUART and NANCY O. LURIE, eds.
1968   The American Indian today. Deland: Everett-Edwards.

LILJEBLAD, SVEN
1957   Indian peoples of Idaho. Mimeographed volume for study only; reproduced at Idaho State University, Pocatello.

LOWIE, ROBERT H.
1909   The Northern Shoshone. Anthropological Papers of the American Museum of Natural History 2(2):169-306.

1915   Dances and societies of the Plains Shoshoni. *Anthropological Papers of the American Museum of Natural History* 11(10):813-822.

1919   The Sundance of the Wind River Shoshoni and Ute. *Anthropological Papers of the American Museum of Natural History* 16:405-410.

1924a   Notes on Shoshonean ethnography. *Anthropological Papers of the American Museum* 20:185-314.

1924b   Shoshonean tales. *Journal of American Folklore* 37: 92-200.

1930   The kinship terminology of the Bannock Indians. *American Anthropologist* 32:294-299.

LUNDSGAARDE, HENRY P.
1963   A theoretical interpretation of Nez Perce kinship. Unpublished M.S. thesis, University of Wisconsin, Madison.

MADSEN, BRIGHAM D.
1948   The Bannock Indians in northwest history, 1805-1900.

Unpublished Ph.D. dissertation, University of California, Berkeley.

MALOUF, CARLING
1945   The effects of Spanish slavery on the Indians of the intermountain west. *Southwestern Journal of Anthropology* 1:378-391.

1952   Early Kutenay history. *Montana Magazine of History* 2(2):5-10.

MURDOCK, GEORGE PETER
1960   Ethnographic bibliography of North America, 3rd edition. New Haven: Human Relations Area Files.

1967   Ethnographic atlas. Pittsburgh: University of Pittsburgh Press.

MURPHY, ROBERT F. and YOLANDA MURPHY
1960
        Shoshone-Bannock subsistence and society. *Anthropological Records* 16(7):293-338.

NIELSON, JEAN C.
1934   The operations of British fur trading companies in Idaho. Unpublished M.A. thesis, University of Idaho, Moscow.

OSWALT, WENDELL
1966   This land was theirs. New York: John Wiley and Sons.

PALLADINO, LAWRENCE B.
1967   The Coeur d'Alene reservation, and our friends the Coeur d'Alene Indians. Fairfield, Washington: Ye Galleon Press.

PARK, WILLARD Z.
1937   Paviotso polyandry. *American Anthropologist* 39: 366-368.

1938   Shamanism in western North America: a study in cultural relationships. Evanston and Chicago: Northwestern University.

PHINNEY, ARCHIE
1934   Nez Perce texts. *Columbia University Contributions to Anthropology,* No. 25.

RAY, VERNE F.
1936   The Kolaskin cult. *American Anthropologist* 38:67-75.

1937   The bluejay character in the Plateau spirit dance. *American Anthropologist* 39:593-601.

1942   Culture element distribution: Plateau (22). *Anthropological Records* 8(2):99-262.

REICHARD, GLADYS A.
1930   The style of Coeur d'Alene mythology. *Proceedings of the International Congress of Americanists* 24:243-253.

1947   An analysis of Coeur d'Alene Indian myths. *Memoirs of the American Folklore Society,* No. 41.

ROE, FRANK GILBERT
1955   The Indian and the horse. Norman: University of Oklahoma Press.

ROSS, ALEXANDER
1956   The fur traders of the far west. Norman: University of Oklahoma Press.

ROSS, SYLVIA H. and CARL N. SAVAGE
1967   Idaho earth science. *Idaho Bureau of Mines and Geology, Earth Science Series,* No. 1.

SAPIR, EDWARD
1918   Kinship terms of the Kootenay Indians. *American Anthropologist* 20:414-418.

SCHAEFFER, CLAUDE E.
1947   The bear foster parent tale: A Kutenai version. *Journal*

of *American Folklore* 60:286-288.

1952   Molded pottery among the Kutenai Indians. *Montana State University, Anthropology and Sociology Papers,* No. 6.

SCRIMSHER, LEDA SCOTT
1967   Native foods used by the Nez Perce Indians of Idaho. Unpublished M.S. thesis, University of Idaho, Moscow.

SCHWEDE, MADGE L.
1970   The relationship of aboriginal Nez Perce settlement patterns to physical environment and to generalized distribution of food resources. *Northwest Anthropological Research Notes* 4(2):129-135.

SHIMKIN, DEMITRI B.
1939   Some interactions of culture, needs, and personalities among the Wind River Shoshone. Unpublished Ph.D. dissertation, University of California, Berkeley.

1947a   Childhood and development among the Wind River Shoshoni. *Anthropological Records* 5(5):289-325.

1947b   Wind River Shoshone ethnography. *Anthropological Records* 5:245-288.

SKEELS, DELL
1954   A classification of humor in Nez Perce mythology. *Journal of American Folklore* 67:57-63.

SPENCER, ROBERT F., JESSE D. JENNINGS, *et al.*
1965   The Native Americans. New York: Harper and Row.

SPINDEN, HERBERT JOSEPH
1908   The Nez Perce Indians. Memoirs of the American Anthropological Association, No. 2.

STEVENS, HAROLD D.
1965   An analysis of Coeur d'Alene Indian-White inter-relations. Unpublished M.A. thesis, University of

Idaho, Moscow.

STEWARD, JULIAN H.
1936   Shoshoni polyandry. *American Anthropologist* 38: 561-564.

1938a   Basin-Plateau aboriginal sociopolitical groups. *Bureau of American Ethnology, Bulletin* 120.

1938b   Lemhi Shoshoni physical therapy. *Bureau of American Ethnology, Bulletin* 119:177-181.

1955   The Great Basin Shoshonean Indians. *In* Theory of culture change, Julian H. Steward, ed., pp. 101-121 Urbana: University of Illinois.

STEWART, OMER C.
1937   Northern Paiute polyandry. *American Anthropologist* 39:368-369.

1939a   The Northern Paiute bands. *Anthropological Records* 2:127-149.

1939b   Washo-Northern Paiute peyotism. *Proceedings of the (fifth) Pacific Science Congress* 6(4):65-68.

1941   Culture element distributions: Northern Paiute (14). *Anthropological Records* 4(3):361-446.

1944   Washo-Northern Paiute peyotism. *University of California Publications in American Archaeology and Ethnology* 40:63-142.

1966   Tribal distributions and boundaries in the Great Basin. *In* The current status of Anthropological research in the Great Basin, Warren L. d'Azevedo, *et al.*, eds., pp. 167-203.

SWANSON, EARL H., JR.
1958   Problems in Shoshone chronology. *Idaho Yesterdays* 1(4):21-26.

1966   The geographic foundations of desert culture. *In* The current status of anthropological research in the Great Basin, Warren L. d'Azevedo, *et al.*, eds., pp. 137-147.

1970   Languages and cultures of western North America. Pocatello: Idaho State University Press.

TEIT, JAMES A.
1917a   Coeur d'Alene tales. *Memoirs of the American Folklore Society* 11:119-128.

1917b   Pend d'Oreille tales. *Memoirs of the American Folklore Society* 11:114-118.

1930   The Salishan tribes of the western plateaus. *Annual Report of the Bureau of American Ethnology* 45:295-396.

TEIT, JAMES A., H.D. HAEBERLIN, and H. ROBERTS
1924   Coiled basketry in British Columbia and surrounding regions. *Annual Report of the Bureau of American Ethnology* 41:119-484.

TUOHY, D.R.
1956   Shoshoni wars from Idaho. *Davidson Journal of Anthropology* 2:55-71.

TURNEY-HIGH, HARRY H.
1941a   Ethnography of the Kutenai. *Memoirs of the American Anthropological Association*, No. 56.

1941b   Two Kutenai stories. *Journal of American Folklore* 54:191-196.

UNDERHILL, RUTH M.
1941   The Northern Paiute Indians. *Bureau of Indian Affairs, Sherman Pamphlets* 1:1-78.

1953   Red Man's America. Chicago: University of Chicago Press.

1965   Red Man's Religion. Chicago: University of Chicago

Press.

VOGET, FRED

1948   The diffusion of the Wind River Shoshone Sundance to the Crow Indians of Montana. Unpublished Ph.D. dissertation, Yale University, New Haven.

1950   A Shoshone innovator. *American Anthropologist* 52:53-63.

1953   Current trends in the Wind River Shoshone Sundance. *Bureau of American Ethnology, Bulletin* 151:485-500.

VOGT, HANS

1940   The Kalispel language. Oslo: I Kommisjon Hos Jacob Dybwad.

VRETTOS, LOUIS

1949   The education of Indians with special reference to the Shoshone Indian Reservation in Wyoming. Unpublished M.A. thesis, University of Wyoming, Laramie.

WALKER, DEWARD E., JR.

1964   A survey of Nez Perce religion. New York: Board of National Missions, United Presbyterian Church in the U.S.A.

1966   The Nez Perce sweat bath complex: an acculturational analysis. *Southwestern Journal of Anthropology* 22(2):133-171.

1967a   Mutual cross-utilization of economic resources in the Plateau: an example from aboriginal Nez Perce fishing practices. *Washington State University, Laboratory of Anthropology, Report of Investigations*, No. 41.

1967b   Nez Perce sorcery. *Ethnology* 6(1):66-96.

1967c   An examination of American Indian reaction to proposals of the Commissioner of Indian Affairs for general legislation. *Northwest Anthropological Research Notes, Memoir* 1.

1968a   Conflict and schism in Nez Perce acculturation: a study of religion and politics. Pullman: Washington State University Press.

1968b   Some limitations of the renascence concept in acculturation: the Nez Perce case. *In* The American Indian today, Stuart Levine and Nancy Lurie, eds., pp. 149-163. Deland: Everett-Edwards.

1969   New light on the Prophet Dance controversy. *Ethnohistory* 16(3):245-255.

1970a   Ethnology and history. *Idaho Yesterdays* 14(1):24-29.

1970b   Systems of North American witchcraft and sorcery. *Anthropological Monographs of the University of Idaho,* No. 1.

1971   The emergent Native Americans. Boston: Little, Brown and Company.

WEIL, PETER M.
1965   Political modernization on the Nez Perce Indian Reservation: 1940-1963. Unpublished M.A. thesis, University of Oregon, Eugene.

WHEAT, M.M.
1959   Notes on Paviotso material culture. *Nevada State Museum Anthropological Papers* 1(1):13.

WHITING, BEATRICE B.
1950   Paiute sorcery. New York: *Viking Fund Publications in Anthropology,* No. 15.

WIGHT, E.L., *et al.*
1960   Indian reservations of Idaho, Oregon, and Washington. U.S. Department of the Interior, Bureau of Indian Affairs.

WILSON, E.F.

1890   The Kootenay Indians. *Journal of American Folklore*
3:10-12.

aboriginal: native, original; pertaining to the original inhabitants of a country or place.

adobe: an unfired, sun-dried clay brick.

affinal: related by marriage.

alkaloid: an alkaline organic substance, occurring naturally in plants.

anadromous: going up rivers at certain seasons for breeding, as salmon, etc.

animism: the belief that natural phenomena and objects, such as rocks, trees, wind, etc., are alive and have souls.

antelope *(Antilocapra americana):* taken aboriginally in central and southern Idaho for its flesh, hide, bone, and antlers. It was sometimes important in religion and mythology as a tutelary spirit.

anthropology: a science that studies man's origin, physical and cultural development, and cultural variation. It emerged formally in universities of the Western world shortly after A.D. 1850 and is divided into four main branches — archaeology, physical anthropology, cultural anthropology or ethnology, and linguistics.

archaeology: the branch of anthropology devoted to the study of past cultures through excavation of their material remains.

avoidance: the restriction of social interaction, especially between affinal relatives such as mother-in-law and son-in-law. (See mother-in-law avoidance)

badger *(Taxidea taxus):* found primarily in the central and southern portions of aboriginal Idaho and taken occasionally for its flesh and fur. It was sometimes an important figure in religion and mythology.

bald eagle *(Haliaetus leucocephalus):* found primarily in the northern and central mountains of Idaho and taken for its feathers, bone, and talons primarily by specialists who were often thought to own species. It was usually an important figure in religion and mythology.

band: a territorially based group of related families led by a headman and usually numbering about 30 to 50 persons. The simplest political grouping.

band leader or band chief: a local group leader similar to a headman, whose power lies primarily in his personal qualities and charisma. He has little vested authority and relies primarily on persuasion to administer the band.

beaver (*Castor canadensis*): found in the northern and southern portions of aboriginal Idaho and taken for its fur and flesh. It was sometimes important in religion and mythology.

bilateral kinship: pertaining to descent through both parents. The kinship system of Euro-Americans.

biotic zone — a geographic zone with a distinctive climate, flora and fauna.

bison *(Bison bison)* — aboriginally taken in southeastern Idaho and west as far as Salmon Falls on the Snake River. It was not an important resource until horses were introduced after which time intensive hunting caused its near extinction. Increasingly, the inhabitants of Idaho were forced to hunt it in the plains of Montana and Wyoming. It was a prestige food for many groups and its hams and hides were prized widely, being traded well into central and western Oregon and Washington. It was often important in religion and mythology.

bitterroot *(Lewisia rediviva)*: low-growing perennial herb with brightly colored white to pink flowers that appear in early spring. The roots have a black outer covering and white meat. They are often dug in May during the flowering season when the black outer surface of the root is easily removed. Its nutrients are similar to those of brown rice except it is lower in iron and higher in calcium and phosphorous. It was used primarily by groups in northern and central Idaho who traveled great distances to dig it.

black bear *(Ursus americanus)*: occurred widely throughout the mountainous portions of aboriginal Idaho. It is smaller than the grizzly bear and lacks it ruff or mane. It ranges in color from black to brown and cinnamon. It was taken regularly for its flesh, fur, teeth, and claws, and was often a major figure in religion and mythology.

blackberry *(Rubus ursinus)*: has white flowers and long, arching stems. The stems and underside of the leaves have curving spur-like stickers about ⅜ of an inch long. This succulent black fruit grows best in moist areas in partial shade and was eaten throughout aboriginal Idaho.

black hawthornberry *(Crataegus douglasi)*: tall, tree-like shrubs with thorns an inch or more long. The leaves are simple, oval-shaped with serrated edges. Hawthornberries were gathered in August and September mostly in mountainous areas.

black moss: see pine moss

black-tailed deer *(Odocoileus hemionus columbianus)*: a variety of mule deer having a black tail. Its thick hide was very durable when tanned.

blind: a lightly built structure of brush or other natural cover behind which hunters conceal themselves in hunting game. Blinds and decoys were used extensively in aboriginal Idaho in the pursuit of game.

blueback salmon *(Oncorhynchus nerka)*: also known as sockeye salmon and red salmon. One of the primary fish taken during annual runs in the warmer months by the aboriginal peoples of Idaho. Its flesh was dried and sometimes pulverized into a form of pemmican. Salmon often figured importantly in religion and mythology.

blueberry: the edible, usually bluish berry of various heath-type shrubs of the genus *Vaccinium*. It was valued as a delicacy and eaten in season as well as dried for consumption during the winter.

bluebird: any of several small songbirds of the genus *Sialia* having predominantly blue plumage. Taken for its flesh, particularly in the Great Basin.

bobcat *(Lynx rufus)*: inhabited most of aboriginal Idaho but was more common in the central and southern portions of the state. It was taken primarily for its fur and was occasionally mentioned in religion and mythology. Also called lynx.

bridewealth: gifts given to a woman's family at the time of her marriage, usually given by her husband and his kinsmen.

brown bear: a variety of the American black bear, having a brownish coat. (See black bear)

cache: a hidden storage place for food and other provisions, usually in the ground. Dried meat, berries, roots, nuts, and other commodities were cached for use in the winter by the aboriginal groups in Idaho. Temporary caches were also in use during all seasons. (See Figure 24)

calendrical rituals: rituals which are performed seasonally, such as Easter in Christian societies.

camas *(Camassia quamash)*: a member of the lily family, it has a round bulb one to one and one-half inches in diameter with a dark outer coating and white meat resembling an onion. It is found in moist meadows on the prairies and is harvested in mid-July through September after the light blue flowers are gone and the seeds have dropped. Testing shows that although camas is lower in fat than beans and liver, it exceeds both foods in carbohydrates, fiber, ash, and calcium, and is one and one-half times higher in protein than liver and four times higher than beans. It was taken by most aboriginal peoples of northern, central, and the northern portion of southern Idaho.

Canada goose *(Branta canadensis)*: found on larger marshes, lakes and rivers throughout aboriginal Idaho. It was taken for its flesh, bone and feathers, and appears in some myths.

captain: a term adopted by Europeans in the Great Basin to designate the leader of a group, usually the oldest able male in the group. (See band leader and headman)

caribou *(Rangifer tarandus)*: taken occasionally by aboriginal peoples of northernmost Idaho. It was not an important resource.

charisma: an aura of extraordinary power and magnetism.

chief: the political leader of a tribe, as among horse cultures of the Great Plains. Such chiefs were largely absent in aboriginal Idaho, where political leaders were more often headmen.

chinook salmon *(Oncorhynchus tshawytscha)*: also known as tyee salmon and king salmon. The most preferred fish taken annually during runs in the warmer months by the aboriginal peoples of Idaho. It was used in the same manner as the blueback salmon and was important in religion and mythology.

chipmunk *(Eutamias)*: found primarily in most of aboriginal Idaho and sometimes taken for its flesh in southern Idaho. It was important in some myths.

chokecherry *(Prunus virginiana)*: a large, tree-like shrub ranging from ten to twenty feet high. The fruit, gathered throughout most of aboriginal Idaho, is round, about three-eights of an inch in diameter, and when ripe is bright shiny red to black. Chokecherries were gathered in late September primarily in the lower elevations.

collateral: referring to relationship through horizontal or sidewise kinship links. Uncles, aunts, cousins, etc., are collateral relatives.

composite band: a territorially based, culturally similar, politically unified group of bands usually led by a temporary leader who acts in the name of a temporary council composed primarily of headmen drawn from the bands which make up a composite band.

conjugal: having to do with marriage.

consanguine: of the same blood, i.e., pertaining to a genetic relationship.

cottontail rabbit: any of several North American rabbits of the genus *Sylvilagus* having a fluffy white tail. They were found throughout aboriginal Idaho and were important in some myths.

cottonwood mushroom *(unidentified)*: gathered during the warm season and often grows on dead stumps of cottonwood trees. Most groups of aboriginal Idaho made some use of mushrooms.

council of leaders (sometimes simply "council"): the major political body among tribal groups, consisting of the leaders and other outstanding people. It directed the collective affairs of the group.

coup: an attested deed of valor among the Plains Indians. It consisted of touching one's enemy without causing harm, or any daring escapade which proved one's bravery.

coup counting: the social practice of publicly reciting heroic deeds performed in battle.

courtesy chief: an honorary title bestowed on outstanding warriors. They often were part of the council of leaders.

cow-parsnip *(Heracleum lanatum)*: an herb three to five feet tall. The large, three-lobed leaves are wooly and the stem terminates in umbels of white flowers. The succulent stem was eaten in the spring and is similar to celery, although it is decidedly higher in all nutrients tested except iron. Most tribes ate this plant occasionally.

coyote *(Canis latrans)*: aboriginally found in the central and southern parts of Idaho. Normally, it was the major figure in myths.

crier or herald: the assistant who announced the decisions of the council or leaders of the group to the public.

cradleboard: a leather-covered, oval-shaped board to which is attached a leather container in which babies are carried. (See Figure 68)

culture: the integrated sum total of attitudes, learned behavior traits, and material products characteristic of a society.

culture area: a geographical territory within which the cultures tend to be similar in some significant aspects, e.g., the Great Basin.

culture complex: an integrated system of culture traits organized about some central theme, e.g., the Plains Indian horse complex.

culture pattern: the accepted forms of behavior either laid down by a society or manifested in the customary actions of its members.

culture trait or element: the smallest unit of learned behavior or material product in a society.

currant *(Ribes)*: reaches a height of four to ten feet. Its leaves are small, lobed, and its stems are free of thorns. Its blooms are yellow and tubular shaped. When ripe the fruit is bright yellow to orange in color. One variety of currants is found at higher altitudes and has a bland flavor, whereas a sweet variety grows along streams and rivers in the valleys. They are ripe in August and September and were picked by most aboriginal groups in Idaho.

cutthroat trout *(Salmo clarkii)*: a spotted trout having a reddish streak on each side of the throat, one of several varieties of trout taken in aboriginal Idaho.

deadfall: a type of trap so constructed that a weighted lever, rock, or ceiling drops on the victim when released by a trigger. (Figure 40) decoy: an object designed to entice game into a trap or within range of weapons. Many types were used in aboriginal Idaho. (Figure 52)

dialect: the form or variety of a spoken language peculiar to a region, community, social or occupational group. Linguists regard dialects as being, to some degree, mutually intelligible, while "languages" are mutually unintelligible.

diffusion: a process wherein culture traits or complexes spread from one society to another. The Plains horse complex "diffused" to the tribes of Idaho.

digging stick: a curved, pointed stick used to dig up roots and occasionally small burrowing mammals. (See Figure 23)

dip net: a net used to dip salmon from streams, especially at rapids and falls. (See Figures 38 and 39)

dipping platform: a platform constructed on the side of a stream or river from which fish are caught with dip nets. (See Figure 38)

dog salmon *(Oncorhynchus keta)*: also known as chum salmon. One of the primary fish taken during annual runs in the warmer months by the aboriginal people of Idaho and used in the same manner as the chinook salmon. All varieties of salmon were mentioned in myths, but not as often as land animals.

dolly varden trout *(Salvelinus malma)*: a red-spotted trout; the name alludes to its bright coloring. One of several varieties of trout taken in aboriginal Idaho.

dove: any bird of the family *Columbidae*, usually the smaller species with pointed tails. Although difficult to catch, its flesh was prized.

duck: any of numerous wild or domesticated web-footed swimming birds of the family *Anatidae*, especially of the genus *Anas* and allied genera. Several varieties of wild ducks were taken on lakes and rivers in aboriginal Idaho.

earth lodge: a house built wholly or partially of sod, or a

framework covered with dirt. (See Figures 58 and 59)

ecology: the study of the relationships between things and their environments. Cultural ecology is a science which analyzes the cultural patterns of a society in terms of its adaptation to a particular environment.

elderberry *(Sambucus cerulea)*: a small shrub with tender, pithy stalks. The berries, blue and about one-eighth inch in diameter, were gathered throughout much of aboriginal Idaho in late August and early September. The best were found in lowlands. Another variety, the mountain elderberry *(Sambucus melanocarpa)*, is smaller and was not often eaten.

elk *(Cervus elaphus)*: aboriginally hunted over most of Idaho for its flesh, hide, bones, hoofs, and antlers. It was a major resource for most groups except those in desert areas, and often figured prominently in religion and myths.

elk thistle *(Cirsium scariosum)*: a greyish-green plant usually found growing alone in mountain meadows. It tapers slightly from the bottom to the top and may reach a height of three to four feet. White to purple blooms are surrounded by deeply dissected leaves. The stems were peeled and eaten fresh by most inhabitants of aboriginal central and northern Idaho.

endogamy: a rule or practice whereby a person must marry within his or her social group. The particular *group* varies among societies, thus, there are many forms of endogamy.

ethnocentrism: the belief in the inherent superiority of one's own group and culture accompanied by a feeling of contempt for other groups and cultures.

ethnology: a branch of anthropology which analyzes cultures, especially in regard to their historical development and the similarities and dissimilarities between them.

Euro-American: refers to the European-derived societies of the Americas.

exogamy: a rule or practice whereby a person must marry

outside his or her social group. As in the case of endogamy, the composition of the *group* varies between societies.

extended family: a three-generation family containing grandparents, parents, grandchildren, and occasional distant relatives.

fall trap: a large, basket-like device for catching fish as they swim downriver. (See Figure 15)

family: an organized social group formed through marriage.

family, nuclear: the two-generation family containing one set of parents, their children, and occasional distant relatives. The common Euro-American domestic family unit.

fatherhood, social: the institution whereby the adult male who is the husband of a child's mother stands in the functional relationship of fatherhood to the child, regardless of their biological relationship.

fireberry *(Vaccinium scoparium)*: also called grouseberry or whortleberry, these were picked in the mountains, usually in open areas. They were eaten only occasionally by groups traveling through the mountains in late summer.

first fruits ceremony: a group ritual of thanksgiving held each spring during the root harvest. Designed to ensure the continued abundance of fish, game, roots, and other food resources.

first salmon ceremony: a group ritual held in the spring when the first salmon were caught. It was thought to ensure future abundance of salmon. During the ceremony, the salmon is welcomed much like a visiting dignitary.

genealogical: through the means of a genealogy or family tree.

golden eagle *(Aquila chrysaetos)*: occurred throughout aboriginal Idaho but particularly in the northern area. It was taken by specialists for its feathers, bone, and talons. It was an important figure in religion and mythology.

gooseberry: the small, edible, acid, globular fruit or berry of certain prickly shrubs of the genus *Ribes*. Like the blueberry, it was eaten in season as well as dried for winter consumption throughout aboriginal Idaho.

gopher: any of several ground squirrels of the genus *Spermophilus*. It was sometimes taken for its meat, especially by the Paiute and prehorse Shoshone-Bannock.

grizzly bear *(Ursus arctos)*: was widespread in aboriginal Idaho and occasionally taken for its flesh, fur, teeth, and claws. It was a major figure in religion and mythology.

ground hog: see woodchuck.

ground squirrel *(Spermophilus)*: found in much of aboriginal Idaho, particularly in the south, and taken for both its flesh and fur.

guide chief: an assistant leader who organized community activities.

head chief: the highest ranking tribal leader, most common in groups having broad political integration.

headman: the political leader of a band who possesses little power over the band members.

hazelnut: the nut of a shrub of the family *Betulaceae*, it was taken as a delicacy throughout aboriginal Idaho.

heron *(Ardea herodias)*: found throughout Idaho in marshes, ponds, and streams at lower elevations. It was occasionally taken for its flesh, bone and feathers and appeared occasionally in the mythology of some groups.

historic period: roughly after A.D. 1800 in Idaho.

horned owl *(Bubo virginianus)*: a chiefly nocturnal bird of prey having a broad head with large eyes that are usually surrounded by disks of modified feathers and directed forward. They feed on mice, small birds, and reptiles. They were sometimes feared as omens of bad luck in aboriginal Idaho.

huckleberry *(Vaccinium membranaceum)*: a black-purple bell-shaped berry with a sweet pleasant flavor, many tiny seeds, and a distinctive odor. They were gathered in the mountains in late July or early August and eaten fresh or dried in the sun.

humpback salmon *(Oncorhynchus gorbuscha)*: also known as pink salmon. One of the primary fish taken during annual runs in the warmer months by the aboriginal peoples of Idaho. It was used in the same way as the chinook salmon.

hunt leader: a leader in charge of larger, organized hunting activities of the community, such as the bison hunts and communal drives of the Nez Perces and Coeur d'Alenes. The general term includes such special hunting leaders as the duck hunting leader, deer hunting leader, etc.

Indian potato *(Helianthus)*: probably the giant sunflower, a hardy, perennial herb growing nearly twelve feet high and having stiff, hairy stems, hairy leaves, and yellow flower heads nearly three inches wide. It has a large, edible, tuberous root, and was occasionally eaten in northern and southern Idaho.

infanticide: the killing of infants. In most cases this practice serves as a means of controlling population growth in an area with scant food resources.

institution, social: a complex of behavior patterns organized about some dominant interest of a society. Societies are comprised of economic, political, religious, family and other institutions.

isolate (language): a language which has no known connections with any other language.

jack rabbit *(Lepus)*: aboriginally it was found in the southern portion of the state and was a major food resource taken mostly in communal drives for its flesh and fur. It was important in some myths.

joking relationship: a relationship of privileged familiarity or joking between certain persons in a society, most often between a husband and his sisters-in-law or a wife and her brothers-in-law. This pattern of behavior usually anticipates marriage. (See levirate and sororate)

kangaroo rat *(Dipodomys ordi)*: found in the southernmost portion of aboriginal Idaho and taken for its flesh and fur.

kinship system: the complex system of interpersonal relationships arising from marriage and descent.

kouse *(Lomatium cous)*: a white-meated, tuberous bulb which may be eaten either raw or cooked. Dug in May, it grows on rocky slopes of hills in areas where there is not much vegetation. Nutritionally, it is a concentrated source of energy, and when compared to parsnip, which it resembles in flavor, it is superior in all respects with the exception of iron. It was taken by most aboriginal peoples of northern, central, and the northern portion of southern Idaho.

lake trout *(Salvelinus namaycush)*: a large, fork-tailed trout, one of several varieties of trout taken in aboriginal Idaho.

lamprey *(Lampetra tridentata)*: caught seasonally during annual runs by most of the aboriginal inhabitants of Idaho who had access to rivers. It was regarded as a delicacy.

language: a group of mutually intelligible dialects spoken by a social group usually possessing a common culture.

language family: a genetically (historically) related group of languages.

language stock: a group of genetically (historically) related language families.

lean-to: a rectangular structure with a sloping roof, often open on the sides, especially in summer. The basic design of many dwellings in aboriginal Idaho.

levirate: the marriage of a woman to her deceased husband's brother(s)

little spotted skunk *(Spilogale putorius)*: occasionally taken in the southern half of aboriginal Idaho for its fur and musk. The musk was used in medicines and huntings, and skunk was often mentioned in myths as a powerful but vain figure.

long-house: a communal dwelling consisting of a wooden framework covered with mats, bark, grasses and earth. (See Figure 25)

loon *(Gavia immer)*: a bird found on most larger lakes in Idaho and occasionally taken for both its flesh and feathers. It was important in some myths.

lynx: see bobcat.

magpie *(Pica pica)*: common throughout Idaho at lower elevations, along stream courses and edges of timber. It was rarely taken for its flesh or feathers but was a principal figure in the myths of several groups.

mallard *(Anas platyrhynchos)*: the most common of the at least twenty different types of ducks taken in aboriginal Idaho for both flesh and feathers. It is occasionally mentioned in myths.

manitou: a term for a supernatural figure or force, especially among Algonquian and other tribes of the eastern United States.

mano: a grinding stone held in the hand and rubbed over a metate.

marmot *(Marmota flaviventris)*: several types were found in the southeastern and southern portions of aboriginal Idaho. They were frequently taken for their flesh and occasionally for their fur. They were occasionally mentioned in myths.

marriage: the social institution that regulates the special relations of a mated pair to each other, their offspring, their kinsmen, and society at large.

marten *(Martes americana)*: taken primarily in mountainous parts of aboriginal Idaho primarily for its fur.

matrilineal: pertaining to descent through the mother and her relatives.

matrilocal: pertaining to the practice whereby a married couple settles in the domicile of the wife's family.

menstrual unit: a small, hemispherical structure occupied by women during their menstrual periods and childbirth.

metate: a flat or grooved grinding stone that functions as a mortar.

mink (Mustela vison): taken primarily for its fur, it was found throughout aboriginal Idaho along streams and lake margins and figured in many myths.

minnow: any fish of the family Cyprinidae, including the carps, goldfishes, and daces. They were eaten only occasionally, primarily in areas of aboriginal Idaho not having salmon runs.

monogamy: marriage of one man to one woman.

moose (Alces alces): taken primarily in the mountainous portions of aboriginal Idaho for its flesh, fur, bone, antlers, and hoofs. It was a major figure in some myths.

mortar: a bowl or stone grinding surface in which seeds were ground with a pestle. Occasionally mortars were made of wood or partly of basketry. (See Figure 42)

mother-in-law avoidance: this custom demands that a son-in-law not speak to his mother-in-law and, in some societies, not even see her. This practice functions to forestall potential conflict between the two people, who often live close together.

mountain goat (Oreamnos americanus): aboriginally taken in mountainous central and northern portions of Idaho, primarily for hide and horns. It was mentioned in some myths.

mountain lion (Felis concolor): aboriginally found throughout the mountainous parts of Idaho and taken primarily for its fur, teeth, and claws. It was often mentioned in myths.

mountain sheep (Ovis canadensis): aboriginally taken throughout the mountainous portions of Idaho primarily for its horns and hide. It was mentioned in some myths.

mouse: any of numerous small rodents of the family *Cricetidae*, especially of the genus *Peromyscus*. They were occasionally taken for food, especially by the Paiute and pre-horse Shoshone-Bannock.

mudhen: any of various marsh-inhabiting birds, especially the American coot. They were hunted for their succulent flesh in aboriginal Idaho.

mule deer *(Odocoileus hemionus)*: found throughout most of aboriginal Idaho and taken for its flesh, hide, bones, antlers, and hoofs. It was a major figure in many myths.

muskrat *(Ondatra zibethica)*: a large, aquatic rodent having a musky odor. Its hide and musk glands were used widely.

mussel *(Lampsilis siliquoidea)*: a succulent shell fish found along streams in Idaho. They were eaten occasionally, primarily in times of famine, when they became an important resource. Mussel shell appears in some myths.

mythology: the traditional oral and/or written literature of a people containing basic beliefs, values, and patterns of thought and usually recounted in a highly stylized manner on special occasions. It is especially important in educating children in non-literate societies.

parfleche: an oblong, rawhide box made by Plains Indians. (See Figure 17)

patrilineal: pertaining to descent through the father and his relatives.

patrilocal: pertaining to the practice whereby a married couple settles in the domicile of the husband's family.

peace chief: a leader whose duties are largely concerned with the direction of civil affairs.

pemmican: meat, often buffalo, that is sun-dried in the form of jerky and pounded and mixed with fat and dried berries. Fish pemmican also was prepared by some groups in aboriginal Idaho.

pestle: a tubular-shaped stone used to grind seeds in a bowl-shaped container. (See Figure 42)

pine moss *(Alectoria jubata)*: a lichen gathered from pine trees in the mountains, because in lower elevations it was thought to be bitter. Two kinds were gathered around the first of July, one dark brown in color and edible, the other light green in color and inedible. Nutritionally compared with plain shredded wheat, it is higher in calcium, fat, fiber, ash, and calories, but lower in protein, carbohydrates, phosphorus, and iron. Most groups used it to some extent as either seasoning or a famine food.

pine nut *(Pinus flexilis)*: a nut secured from long-needled pines, which were parched in ashes. They were an important aboriginal food resource in southern Idaho.

pink salmon *(Oncorhynchus gorbuscha)*: also known as humpback salmon. One of the primary fish taken during annual runs in the warmer months by aboriginal peoples of Idaho and used in the same manner as the chinook salmon. Salmon were important in religion and mythology.

pit dwelling: an earth lodge built over an excavated pit.

pitfall: a concealed pit prepared as a trap for animals.

polyandry: the marriage of a woman to two or more men simultaneously.

polygamy: any multiple marriage.

polygyny: the marriage of a man to two or more women simultaneously.

polygyny, sororal: a form of polygyny in which a man is married to two or more sisters simultaneously.

ponderosa pine bark *(Pinus ponderosa)*: procured and eaten in the early spring when the sap was rising and the tissue still tender. Strips of bark approximately eight to ten inches wide and one foot long were peeled from the pine trees. The inner layer was then peeled off and eaten as a treat. Most groups in central and the northern portion of southern Idaho made use of this food resource.

porcupine *(Erethizon dorsatum)*: found throughout most of aboriginal Idaho and taken occasionally for food but usually for its quills for use in decoration. It was important in some myths.

prairie chicken: either of two birds of the western prairies, *Tympanuchus cupido* (greater prairie chicken) and *T. pallidicinctus* (lesser prairie chicken), having brown, black and white plumage. Also called prairie fowl, prairie grouse. The were hunted widely for their succulent flesh and for their feathers.

prairie dog: any of several gregarious, burrowing rodents of the genus *Cynomys*, having a bark-like cry. They were taken for food by the Paiute and pre-horse Shoshone-Bannock.

prehistoric period: the period preceding the time of written records; roughly before A.D. 1800 in Idaho.

priest: a religious functionary whose supernatural authority is bestowed upon him by a cult or organized church, in contrast to the shaman, who derives his power directly from supernatural sources and consensus of the community at large.

property, communal: property which is owned by the entire community.

ptarmigan *(Lagopus leucurus)*: found at higher elevations in the northern part of aboriginal Idaho. It was not important for food or feathers and was rarely mentioned in myths.

purple gooseberry *(Unidentified)*: occasionally gathered in August and more sour than the red gooseberry.

quail *(Oreortyx pictus)*: resident along the Snake River Canyon and in the eastern half of central Idaho. It was not important as food or in mythology.

raccoon *(Procyon lotor)*: restricted primarily to the southern portion of aboriginal Idaho and unimportant except for occasional mention in myths.

raspberry: the fruit of any of several shrubs of the genus *Rubus*, consisting of small and juicy red, black, or pale yellow berries. They were eaten in season but also dried for winter consumption.

redfish salmon *(Oncorhynchus kennerlyi)*: a type of salmon taken in small numbers in aboriginal Idaho during annual runs in warmer months. It was used in the same way as the chinook salmon.

red fox *(Vulpes vulpes)*: found primarily in the mountainous part of aboriginal Idaho and taken for its fur. It was mentioned in many myths as closely related to Coyote.

red gooseberry: this rare berry found in canyons was gathered in August, but was of little economic importance.

red squirrel *(Tamiasciurus hudsonius)*: found throughout the timbered regions of central and northern Idaho and occasionally taken for its flesh. It was also taken for its fur, but was only rarely mentioned in myths.

red thornberry *(Crataequs columbiana)*: the plant resembles and grows in the same areas as the black thornberry; its berries were gathered in late September and early October.

religion: belief in a superhuman power or powers, which is usually expressed in ceremonials designed to secure individual or group welfare.

robin *(Turdus migratorius)*: a large, American thrush, having a chestnut-red breast and abdomen. It was occasionally hunted for its flesh.

ruffed grouse *(Bonasa umbellus)*: found primarily in forested regions of aboriginal Idaho and taken for its flesh and feathers. It was occasionally mentioned in myths.

sage hen *(Centrocercus urophasianus)*: common in sagebrush areas of southern Idaho and taken regularly for its succulent flesh. It was sometimes mentioned in myths.

scarification: the process of mutilation of the body through the artificial raising of scar tissue.

scraper: an implement with a sharp cutting edge made from bone or stone and used for many purposes, especially to dress hides and smooth shafts. (See Figure 22)

seedbeater: a basketry tool shaped like a tennis racket which was used to shake seeds from plants into a basketry container held underneath. (See Figure 53)

seine: a fishing net which hangs vertically in the water, having floats at the upper edge and sinkers at the lower. Normally it is used by two men who manipulate it by means of poles to which each end is attached. Seines were used throughout aboriginal Idaho to catch smaller fish.

senilicide: the killing of the aged. In most cases it is the aged person who leaves the group or requests to be abandoned, and is necessitated by the fact that he or she becomes a burden on the group when no longer able to contribute to its subsistence. This practice normally occurs only in societies which have a marginal level of subsistence.

serviceberry *(Amelanchier)*: shrubs range in height from three to twenty feet and during the flowering season are covered with a profusion of white five-petaled flowers. The leaves from one to three inches in length, are oval-to-round shaped. The fruit has a tuft on top and several small soft seeds. It is purple to black when mature. It was generally gathered in July on the prairies where they grew best. They are considerably higher than raisins in nutrients when analyzed.

shaman: a religious specialist who has received his power directly from supernatural sources; synonymous with medicine man.

sibling: brother or sister.

silver salmon *(Oncorhynchus kisutch)*: also known as coho salmon. One of the primary fish taken during annual runs in the warmer months by aboriginal peoples of Idaho. It was used in the same way as the chinook salmon.

sinew: a tendon. The tendons of game animals were used in the manufacture of bows and as lashing cords where great strength was required.

snare: a device consisting of a noose for capturing birds or small animals. A simple trigger mechanism activates the snare when it is touched by an animal.

snowdrops *(Orogenia linearifolia)*: flourishes on warm sunny slopes. As snow recedes, it sends up an umbel of white flowers before the leaves appear. Foliage is seldom over four to five inches. The bulb is round, about one inch in diameter, with dark and white meat. It may be eaten either raw or cooked and is a good source of calcium; 100 grams contain more than one and one-half times the daily requirement. Compared with the potato, it excels in all respects except iron. It was used by most aboriginal peoples in northern, central, and the northern portion of southern Idaho.

snowshoe rabbit *(Lepus)*: occurred primarily in the northern and central portions of the state and was prized for its fur by the aboriginal peoples of these regions. It was regularly mentioned in myths.

snowy egret *(Egretta thula)*: occasionally taken for its feathers and bone by aboriginal peoples of Idaho.

society: a population of humans living as a distinct entity and possessing a distinct culture.

society, ceremonial: a fraternity or association whose membership and activities are shrouded in secrecy. Often called secret society.

sororate: the marriage of a man to his deceased wife's sister(s).

splitting wedge: a tool usually made of elk horn and used to split logs.

spring-pole trap: see snare.

spruce grouse *(Canachites canadensis)*: hunted in northern Idaho, especially by the Kutenai.

squawfish *(Ptychocheilus oregonensis)*: taken primarily by

groups in central and northern Idaho and occasionally mentioned in myths.

steelhead trout: a silvery rainbow trout that migrates to the sea before returning to fresh water to spawn. It was taken in most of central and northern Idaho, primarily during the winter months.

sturgeon *(Acipenser transmontanus)* larger, and *(Acipinser medirostris)* smaller: a large fish found on the Snake River and occasionally taken by groups such as the Nez Perces. Its flesh, skin and bones were prized and it was important in certain myths.

sucker *(Catostomus commersoni)*: several types were taken but they were less desirable than salmon, steelhead, or whitefish. They were often taken in winter and figured in some myths.

sunflower, balsamroot *(Balsamorhiza sagittata)*: a small sunflower with gray-green foliage. Long, smooth, and arrow-shaped leaves are basal and surround the leafless stems from which the bright yellow flowerheads originate. Both the seeds and stem were eaten by most aboriginal peoples of Idaho.

sweat house: a small, hemispherical structure used for sweatbathing. Sweatbathing was thought to produce strong bodies, cure illness, and bring good luck. The sweatbath worked through heat from heated rocks that were sprinkled with water to make steam.

syringa: any shrub of the genus *Philadelphus*. It was primarily used in the manufacture of bows and arrows.

taboo: a socially forbidden act which is punishable primarily by supernatural means.

thimbleberry *(Rubus parviflorus)*: an erect shrub from three to four feet tall with leaves that are five-lobed and stems having no spines. It produces large, red, cup-like fruit which was eaten widely in aboriginal Idaho.

tipi: a conical skin tent; sometimes covered by woven mats in aboriginal Idaho. (See Figures 45 and 55)

topography: the physical contours of the earth's surface and/or the study of it.

travois: a carrying device of two poles hitched to a draft animal like the tongues of a buggy. The free ends of the travois drag along the ground. (See Figure 20)

tribe: a society unified primarily by kinship ties and usually possessing a distinctive language or dialect and a distinctive culture.

trickster: a character in mythology who alters the order of things by tricking men or animals into choices or circumstances that they do not expect or desire. Coyote was the trickster in most mythologies of aboriginal Idaho.

tumpline: a line, generally of cloth, worn about the forehead and used to support objects being carried on the back and shoulders. Usually associated with women.

tutelary spirit: a supernatural being usually seen in a vision and believed to grant special powers or abilities.

unilateral kinship: pertaining to descent through one parent only, either the father (patrilineal) or mother (matrilineal).

vision quest: usually a formal vigil kept by an adolescent accompanied by fasting, exercise and prayer in order to secure visionary encounter with a tutelary spirit.

wada (Suaeda depressa): this was a staple seed crop taken in large quantities by the Paiute and Shoshone-Bannock for winter consumption.

war leader or war chief: a leader who was in charge of raiding and defensive activities of the community. He administered discipline within some tribes and took an active role in directing buffalo hunts out on the western plains.

weasel (Mustela): found in the northern part of aboriginal Idaho and taken primarily for its fur. It was important in some myths.

weir: a fence made of brush and poles set in a stream for catching fish. Weirs were used extensively in aboriginal Idaho during the fishing seasons. (See Figure 13)

whitefish *(Coregonus williamsonii)*: taken regularly among most aboriginal groups in Idaho but not in as large amounts as the various types of salmon.

white-tailed deer *(Odocoileus virginianus)*: a common North American deer having a tail with a white underside. It was taken in most parts of aboriginal Idaho.

wild carrot *(Daucus pusillus)*: a smooth, slender, erect herb from one to four feet high with relatively few pinnate leaves and an umbel of white flowers. The smooth, brown-skinned bulbs have white meat, are two to three inches long, and one-half inch in circumference. Nutritionally, when compared to the carrot, it is exceedingly richer in all nutrients except iron. Other so-called wild carrots, *Lomatim dissectum* and *Lomatim salmoniflorum*, are used as medicines. These were used by most aboriginal inhabitants of Idaho.

wild celery *(Lomatium grayi)*: appears in the spring, with large feathery leaves which are all basal. They reach a height of one to two feet. Just before the umbels of yellow flowers appear, the covering of the stem is easily removed and is eaten raw like a sunflower stalk. Most aboriginal groups ate this occasionally.

wild onion *(Allium geyeri)*: the leaves are basal, round or grass-like and extend one-half to three-fourths the length of the flowering stem. Plants vary from a height of one to one and one-half feet.

wild potato *(Lomatium canbyi)*: one of the first plants harvested in the spring. It bloomed in late March and early April primarily on hillsides. It was eaten by most peoples of central and northern Idaho.

wild strawberry *(Fragaria)*: gathered and eaten fresh in most of aboriginal Idaho.

wolf *(Canis lupus)*: aboriginally found in the mountainous parts of the state and was an important figure in some myths. Its fur and teeth were prized.

woodchuck *(Marmota flaviventris)*: a stocky, burrowing North American marmot that hibernates in the winter. It was taken for food, especially in southern Idaho. Also called ground hog.

woodpecker: any of numerous birds of the family *Picidae* having a hard, chisel-like bill which they use to extract insects from trees. Their stiff tail feathers assist them in climbing. They were often taken for their brightly colored plumage.

wood rat *(Neotoma)*: a large, bushy-tailed rodent noted for carrying away small articles which it stores in its nest. It is sometimes called pack rat and was taken for food by the Paiute and pre-horse Shoshone-Bannock.

xerophytic: drought-resistant vegetation, such as sagebrush, commonly found in desert environments.

yellow bell *(Fritillaria pudica)*: gathered early in the year during periods of famine. It was eaten raw. The roots are very small, about the width of a pencil in diameter.